EVEREST, A COCKPIT AN

SHEILA DYSON was born and raised in Ireland, completed teacher training in London and moved north to live and work in Sheffield. While a student she developed a passion for mountaineering that was to take her around the world. In 1984 she married Cyril Dyson, a Sheffield climber, whose death in 1992 triggered a determination in Sheila to fulfil three dreams she had since childhood. Now she lectures and writes about her experiences as well as working as a home-tutor. She lives in Sheffield.

Cover picture: Mount Everest taken from summit of Mera Peak in background, G-AJIT, the Auster J, in middle ground, Sheila Dyson on summit of Mount Vinson in foreground.   *Compilation: S. Cullen*

Everest, a Cockpit and Antarctica

THREE DREAMS FULFILLED

Sheila Dyson

Red Grouse Publishing

Red Grouse Publishing
PO Box 3614
Sheffield, S12 2WU
Tel 0114-2642773

First published in Great Britain by Red Grouse Publishing, 2004

ISBN 0-9547746-0-4

Typeset in Times New Roman
Printed and bound in Great Britain
by J.W. Northend, Sheffield

For Cyril

ACKNOWLEDGEMENTS

I would like to thank my mother-in-law, Mary Dyson, for her unfailing love and support, Colin and Pat Crooks for their lifelong friendship, Bill and Margaret Nicholson for theirs, and Sue Cullen for the days she has spent with me in the hills.

I thank Ian Drake for his persistence in teaching me to fly, Martyn Webster for the flying journeys that we made together, Andy Broom for his guidance in Nepal, and Anne Kershaw and Dave Hahn of Adventure Network International for their support and guidance in Antarctica.

I thank Barry Nicholls and members of Abbeydale Writers in Sheffield for their support in the preparation of this book, Katy Carter for editing it, Sue Cullen for proof reading it and, with Mary Dyson, designing the cover, Brian Lewis for his advice and guidance, and Clare Jenkins for her encouragement to pursue the project.

Thanks also for the lines from *High Flight*, reproduced with permission from John Magee the Pilot Poet published by This England Magazine, PO Box 52, Cheltenham, GL50 1YQ.

Sheila Dyson
May, 2004

ILLUSTRATIONS

MAPS

CONTENTS

Prologue

March 1992

We travel in convoy through the western suburbs of Sheffield and on to Hathersage in the Peak District. Up the hill behind Hathersage is Stanage Edge, a gritstone edge some four miles long, and a place where the country's finest climbers cut their teeth. About halfway along Stanage is Robin Hood's Cave and, below that, a mountain rescue hut. We come to a final halt in the car park nearby.

I open the boot lid and extract the black and blue rucksack which contains the purpose of the journey. Then I lead the way up the trail I reconnoitred a few days earlier. Focusing on the task ahead of me, I slowly advance up the trail to a plantation surrounded by a gritstone wall. With a desperate energy I stride up the flagstone trail to the top of Stanage Edge and turn right along the trail into a gusting head wind. Soon I reach the fence post that is my landmark for Robin Hood's Cave. We descend into it and make for the balcony at the front.

The moment has come. I say, "Let's have a minute's silence for Cyril." We bow our heads and think of the big, warm, bearded character who had been a friend to all of us and a husband to me. I speak again: "Let's have three cheers for Cyril!"

Robin Hood's Cave resounds with our yells. Then I open the rucksack and lift out the bronze plastic urn. I unscrew the cap and, carefully tipping the urn over, I pour some of the fine, grey dust on to the floor of the cave. Cyril will rest in the place where he'd spent happy nights as a young climber, coming back from the pub at Hathersage with three portions of fish and chips to soak up a night's beer.

But there is more to it than beer and chips. I turn to the front of the cave with the bulk of the ash still in the urn. I lean over the balcony and pour the rest over the edge on to the soil of Derbyshire. The wind takes us by surprise and a gust blows ash back on us. I can almost hear Cyril chuckle as I say to the others, "At this rate we'll all have eaten a bit of Cyril!" We laugh at the thought as we dust ourselves down. I take a last look out on the wet and windblown day and get ready to leave the cave. Then we do what Cyril would have done: we retire to the nearest decent pub and have lunch by a roaring fire.

I know that Cyril will forever be a part of the landscape that he loved.

PART ONE

The Himalayas

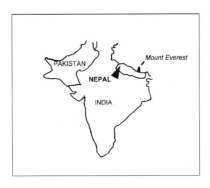

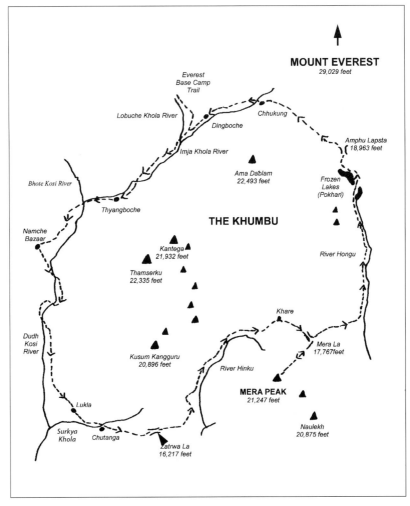

Early Days

The early days of grief for Cyril carried bouts of pain that were almost beyond bearing; in between came flashes of rage. A deep, white-burning anger took root inside me. Its strength and frequency shocked me profoundly, but soon it became my protection. Weeks after I had scattered his ashes, the loss of Cyril hit me with full force and I had no defence against the awful wound inside me except my rage and anger. If anyone came near the wounded part of me, I would lash out in pure rage. It was my only defence. Inevitably, I sank into a severe depression. My only achievement that year was to survive.

The first anniversary brought a surprise. I visited Robin Hood's Cave and found that the dreadful pain of the past year had lessened. I thought of the Victorian wisdom of a year's mourning and as I drove back to Sheffield from Stanage Edge, I felt a small flicker of hope for better times. And I started to think about what I was going to do with the rest of my life.

In the midst of the turmoil, I rid myself of three things which were no longer of any use to me. The first was my old social life which became too painful to engage in on my own. The second was my lecturing job at a local college. Administration and bureaucracy were two irrelevancies I could do without. The third was my Catholic religion. I could find no answer to the question: why? On Sundays at Mass I raged at God. I could not reconcile the idea of a loving God with the anguish I was enduring. The so-called all powerful, loving, merciful God had nothing to do with me. On the day I made a conscious decision to withdraw from the church, a great weight fell from my shoulders.

The biggest factor in my life was that I was fundamentally alone, apart from a close relationship with my mother-in-law. All I had was my own life, and I no longer took it for granted. That being the case, I decided the only thing to do was live it to the full and that meant doing the things I really wanted. When I asked myself what they were, the answers came back loud and clear: to see Mount Everest, to be a pilot, and to make a journey on the ice cap of Antarctica. These were the things I had always said I would do if I could do anything I liked and, when I reflected on them, I recalled the moments in my early life when the dreams had come into being. They linked up a long-past childhood with my new circumstances.

I grew up in Dublin in the mid-1950s and 1960s, the third child of an English father from Cheshire and an Irish mother from County Kildare. They were both Catholic and, in different ways, exerted a profound influence on the way I lived. My father brought Victorian attitudes, with all their limitations, to our home; my mother's contribution was a good dose of Irish rebellion, acquired from a large family on a large farm. It was an opposition that worked well for them but had a contradictory effect on their children.

On the one hand, I learned early from my father the limited expectations of a female child; on the other, I gained a sense of adventure and curiosity from my mother. My father expected women and girls to be subservient to male needs, obedient and dutiful. But even when I fulfilled this cold, unsatisfying role, there was no reward of affection or fun. All I ever felt towards my father was fear and loneliness – fear when he shouted or threatened corporal punishment if things weren't done according to how he wanted, and loneliness because he rarely expressed any kind of affection. I grew up believing that men had no feelings except anger because I never saw the men in my life expressing anything else. In contrast, I had a warm, comfortable relationship with my mother and I loved our holidays on my grandparents' farm in County Kildare, where the repressive tensions of my father were left behind in Dublin. I played out in the fields and farmyard and invariably ended up with mud or cowpat attached to my dress, my hair ribbons lost and in some kind of scrape. On one such occasion I left the paddock gate open and the dairy herd came to visit while we ate dinner around the large kitchen table but, whatever I did, I was always forgiven by my aunts and uncles. I always cried when I had to go home.

Life in Dublin was different. Every day there were chores for my sister, Anne, and myself to do but never, it seemed, for my brothers. My growing but unconscious resentment started to express itself. My parents gave me dolls to play with and I stabbed the eyes out of every one of them. I knew, probably from the age of four, that things were different for boys and that what little girls did was despised. I started to reject the girlish things and was intensely curious to see what the males in our household thought was better. I became a tomboy and spent much of my time in the company of my two brothers, Johnny and Tony, and found a world of physical movement and adventure, fighting, fun and trouble. I was often the only girl amidst a gang of boys and I remember getting into more than one sand fight on Sandymount Strand in Dublin and hearing the boys of the other gang shouting, "Get the girl!" They didn't succeed.

I was disappointed when I turned into a real girl at the age of 12 but was delighted to discover sport and the fact that I was good at it, especially hockey, swimming and rounders. I played hockey on the first eleven at my convent school and became a competitive club swimmer. My father had a conflict over my sport – he was pleased that I was a competent sportswoman but irritated that it would distract me from the long-term destiny of a domestic role. I heard him speak disparagingly of a girl I knew who he thought would be a hit at the local tennis club but hopeless in the office. The apparent rejection of the joyful things in life for girls added to my unspoken resentment and rebellion, and the desire to be a pilot rose directly out of this.

At the age of nine, I found myself in the company of my parents and my older brother, Johnny, on a return flight from Manchester to Dublin. We had been to visit my paternal aunts (who never gave me that wonderful feeling of happiness that my Irish aunts gave me on the farm) and were flying home. I sat with my mother and Johnny sat in front of us with my father. A few minutes into the flight, the stewardess came down the aisle and said to my father, "Would the boy like to come and see the cockpit?" "Yes!" I yelled inside my head but, of course, no one could hear me and no one asked me. My brother was escorted to the cockpit and came back looking bored. I knew there was no point in speaking up – little girls weren't interested in aeroplanes. But from that moment, I had a burning desire to see a cockpit and, for days after we were back in Dublin, every time I heard an aeroplane I'd rush out into the garden and look up at the sky. I'd imagine myself on the aeroplane and wonder if it was going to Manchester. I never lost the desire to be in the pilot's seat, but it remained my secret, because no one in my family would ever understand.

I left my convent school at the age of 18 and went to work in the invoice department of a building contractor's company in Dublin. What I really wanted to do was to teach physical education, but when I told my parents this they said they couldn't afford it. So I settled into office work and played hockey at weekends, eventually representing my province, Leinster. I also qualified as a swimming teacher at Loughborough Summer School and life had, at least, its sporting consolations.

It was around this time that I acquired my ambition to see Mount Everest. It happened in the most ordinary of ways, but my restless mind was ready for it. I was walking up Claremont Road, where I lived, on the way to the public library when I met two sisters, Jane and Mary Bruton, whom I'd known at school.They were a few years older than me. I greeted them and asked casually, "Been away on holiday?" Jane's answer floored me. "Yes," she said, pleased to be asked, "I've been on an overland trip to India." My ears strained as she went on, "I went in a minibus with eight other people and we went through 17 countries. It took us two months and we camped every night." I don't know if she knew the effect she was having, but I felt my mouth drop open. To me, visiting another country, any country, was a great adventure, but to visit 17 in two months was too much. She added as a finishing touch, "Then I joined a trek in Kathmandu and went to Mount Everest Base Camp." By the time I'd mumbled "Goodbye", my heart was pounding and I wanted to make the same journey myself; but as with the flying, I didn't waste my time telling anyone.

At the age of 20 I hit crisis point with my father. His health was deteriorating and my presence in the family home seemed to irritate him greatly. There was no peace between us and even being in the same room caused tension. I became increasingly unhappy and depressed and conceived the idea of emigrating to Canada as a swimming teacher, but that avenue of escape was closed to me when I failed my advanced teacher's certificate at Loughborough Summer School. My frustration reached its high point soon after and, for the first time ever, I stood my ground and had a furious argument with my father. I was more afraid of him destroying my life than of anything he could threaten me with. It was a turning point. Six weeks later, on Friday 26 September 1969, I left work at 5.45 pm and three hours later took the emigrant ship for London.

After that, life could only improve. At first, I worked in the staffing department of Lloyds Bank head office but, eventually, I was accepted for teacher training in physical education at Maria Assumpta College in London. I was glad to be able to do this independently of my father, as I received a full grant from the Inner London Education Authority. During my three years at college, I discovered mountaineering on a trip to Langdale in the Lake District and I was soon hooked. I only went on the trip, in January in the snow, because I fancied a bearded young man at the college next door and wanted him to notice me. The budding romance was a disaster, but I had found something else – the pure beauty of mountains under snow, the freedom and adventure of rock climbing and hill walking and the lively social life that went with them. I wanted more of this and when I left college in 1973, I moved north to live and work in Sheffield.

I joined the Castle Mountaineering Club and found myself in the company of like-minded people. I enjoyed trips to the isles of Skye and Arran off the west of Scotland and was flattered to have a number of male admirers, but the main benefit I gained from the club was the seed of my third dream – to make a journey on the ice cap of Antarctica. A club member, Andy Smith, who had been a base commander for the British Antarctic Survey, gave a slide show and talk in the club house. He showed a slide of a little orange tent pitched in the middle of a glacier. It belonged to two geologists who were making a summer journey on the ice. Immediately, that tent was mine and I could see myself making my own journey. I was 26 years old and my secret dreams now numbered three. Would they ever take me anywhere? Regretfully, I didn't think they would.

Then I met Cyril Dyson, in a room over the bar in the Foresters Arms in Division Street, Sheffield. It was early November 1976 and I had decided to change mountaineering clubs, as my friends in the Castle had moved on. So I went to see what the Parnassus Mountaineering Club would be like. I bought myself a drink in the bar and climbed the narrow stairs that led to the meeting room. I pushed open the door and there was Cyril, sitting opposite with his back to the window and smoking his pipe. From that moment, everything in me said "Yes!"

Our first date was a New Year's Eve party. Cyril called at the house I shared with two other women and we walked to the bus stop. As we waited, he said, "There's another party tomorrow night, will you come to that as well?" A few days later we went walking in the snow along Howden Edge in the Derwent Valley in Derbyshire. From the edge we descended towards Abbey Brook and I struggled after Cyril's tall figure as he broke trail through the snow – knee-deep for him, but it came half way up my thighs. I felt a warm, warm happiness as I followed him and suddenly I thought, "I've hit the jackpot!" I was in love with him.

Cyril was part of my life for 15 years. Our foundation was the integrity that we both found in the mountains. He used to say, "If you want to get to know someone, go camping and walking with them." There is no hiding place in the hills and we experienced a mutual delight with what we found in each other. We made a good mountain team. I guided him over rough ground and in the dark – his eye condition caused him to have tunnel vision and night blindness. He guided me when I was afraid on exposed rock. We had few arguments – our natures blended so comfortably. I was the lively one, always wanting to do things. He was the steady one, who gave me rock-solid support in my ventures; I gave him space and acceptance when he didn't want to join in. Being together was the greatest pleasure in both our lives and we married on 2 August 1984. He was 47 and I was 35. It was a late marriage but we didn't expect it to be a short one. In 1991, Cyril developed mesothelioma, a cancer of the lining of the lung caused by exposure to asbestos. After a desperate fight, he died on 16 February 1992.

The year before Cyril died was a hard one. We both knew his cancer was terminal – there was no cure and no treatment, except to alleviate the symptoms. But the integrity that had brought us together now bound us even tighter. At the end, when all the normal things of life had been destroyed, we were committed to each other with an unbreakable bond which even death could not alter. They were hard times, and the year after his death was harder still. But out of it came, paradoxically, the inspiration to fulfil the three dreams that had been born many years before.

Getting Started

I decided to start with Mount Everest. I put flying aside for the time being as when I told my mother-in-law, Mary, that I was thinking of becoming a pilot, she looked so disgusted and upset I knew I couldn't put her through it. She had just lost her only son and I knew she hated flying. I sensed she had mental images of me mangled in a wreck. I put Antarctica to the bottom of the list as it would be a huge trip and I felt it could wait its turn. So Everest it was to be.

On reflection, it was also the logical choice, mainly because I was mountain fit. I had several months off work after Cyril died because of severe depression and stress and my therapy had been regular hill walking in the Peak District. It is said that bereaved individuals often go looking for the person who has been lost and on the twice weekly 5-6 hour slogs, I sought Cyril. Did I find him? I thought I did. Usually I walked alone and talked to him constantly as I learned to navigate my way through the heather and bracken, up steep hills and along the gritstone edges. I often heard his deep voice in my head as he made dry comments about my navigation skills and how to cope with the feeling of not being certain where I was. That was usually resolved by stopping for a sandwich, a coffee and a good look at the map.

I often thought that Cyril came to me as a bird. More than once, the "go back, go back" of the red grouse roused my attention as I was about to fall into a bog. Sometimes, the lonely call of the curlew brought him to me. He had described it as the loneliest sound in the world, but when

I heard it on the moors, I found it strangely comforting, because I could hear Cyril as well.

Learning to navigate solo gave me the confidence the year after Cyril died to tackle the Cumbrian Way, an 80-mile walk across the Lake District from Ravenglass on the west coast to Appleby in Westmorland. Cyril was with me on that journey. Finding accommodation in a good hotel the night before I started, knowing what to take in my backpack – tent, stove, food, sleeping bag and spare clothing – reading the guide and matching it to the map and the landscape, coping with wet weather and wet tents: these skills were part of Cyril's mountain legacy to me. Whenever things became difficult, I heard his voice.

During this period I also ran the hills of the Peak District, in the company of running friends at Totley Athletics Club in Sheffield. We ran three times weekly in the summer over the hills and trails. I loved running and competing in local fell races. The activity lifted me out of myself, provided me with undemanding company and made me very fit.

I did my research on treks and expeditions to the Himalayas and finally, a trek to Mera Peak, at 21,247 feet the highest trekking peak in Nepal, caught my attention. On it I would have extensive views of Mount Everest, only 12 miles away, and I would have the unexpected bonus of an opportunity to bag a Himalayan peak for myself. Then, because I was travelling so far, I decided to extend the journey for a few weeks so I could spend time in the Kanchenjunga area of eastern Nepal looking at the lives of the people, especially the women. Having spent so much time listening to male mountaineers describe their Himalayan exploits, I was curious to find out what the women of Nepal thought about things. Kanchenjunga appealed – it's the third highest mountain in the world and a stunning backdrop against which to do informal research. When the travel documents arrived at my home in January 1994, pure delight, excitement and adrenalin flushed through me as I skipped, hopped, danced and hugged myself with glee in my lounge. I was going to see Mount Everest.

I told my mother-in-law a few weeks later as we drank tea in her kitchen. She made little response when I told her my plan, but neither did she object. I had the feeling that mountains were more acceptable to her than aeroplanes. Having lived with Cyril's mountaineering and climbing for four decades, she understood how much it had meant to him and now she gave me the same understanding. It was one of the things I loved about her.

Although her name was Mary, I called her Mum. She'd become my second mother the day I married Cyril – my real mother had died six days before. She had the finest qualities any mother-in-law could possess – an ability to keep quiet and to mind her own business. This never stopped her speaking her mind when she thought it was important, but once she had expressed herself, she let the matter drop and didn't interfere. Her qualities of diplomacy would put any Foreign Secretary to shame. After Cyril died, she became even more of a mother to me and I became more of a daughter to her; for years I have referred to her simply as "my mother". Often, I invited her to come and support me at a road race and my running friends envied me my fan club. She'd be waiting on the finish line, cheering me in and bringing out the smelling salts in case I fainted. Then we'd go and share a picnic at a beauty spot on the way home, something she loved doing.

Departure day was set for Friday 29 April 1994. I travelled to Gatwick by coach and dragged my large rucksack and army kit bag into the terminal from which the Royal Nepal Airlines flight would depart. The trekking group and guide had agreed to meet in a particular bar and I sat in the corner looking for people with large rucksacks and kit bags. Eventually, a young couple came in pushing a large trolley piled high with rucksacks. Over the next hour, the rest of the group arrived including Andy Broom, the guide from the Out There Trekking company.

"I can't believe I'm going to the Himalayas!" Eleanor Bailey spoke with enthusiasm and a slight catch in her voice. I knew just what she meant. It was the feeling that we were doing something we had only dreamt about before, and now we were going to the Himalayas ourselves and would be there tomorrow. Like Eleanor, I felt choked at the thought. She introduced me to her partner, Phil Williams.

The flight took off promptly at 8 pm. At Frankfurt we picked up more passengers for the next leg to Dubai. I sat with Phil and Eleanor and learned that he was a policeman and she a nurse. Both were keen mountain walkers. Content, I fell asleep and woke up to a bright morning as the aircraft made its desert approach to Dubai. "The best duty free in the world," I heard Andy say. He went on, "They're strict on security – we won't even be allowed into the airport. They're red hot on drugs and terrorists, but no one ever gets pulled by security …"

As I sat on one of the comfortable seats in the duty free and watched the Arab world go by, I felt the tension of the new and foreign. This was my first time going east and much as the long, white, flowing robes and red and white checkered headgear of the men fascinated me, I was apprehensive, mainly because despite being part of a group, I felt alone. Then it was time to return to the aircraft.

Andy and the rest of the group were ahead of me in the queue as we shuffled towards the security gate. Suddenly, the siren on the electronic gate shrieked and I stood stock still. It was me. Another siren shrieked by the X-ray machine. It was my rucksack. My heart pounded as four security guards surrounded me. I just had a glimpse of Andy looking back anxiously at me before the guards led me away through double doors down a side corridor. Weak at the knees, I managed to walk with them into a room reserved for female body searches.

An Arab woman, wearing a black uniform, sat behind a metal desk and looked up with anticipation as I was escorted in. The four male security guards withdrew and I was left alone facing her. I became aware of a knot of fear in the pit of my abdomen. As the seconds passed, it expanded and crept across my belly. The woman rose from behind the desk and stood in front of me. I had time to take in the black shirt and trousers, the heavy black boots and the revolver in a black holster on her hip. Then I looked her in the eye and every nerve was put on edge by her soulless, empty expression. Looking straight through me, she came close to me and with a curling of her lips to indicate what she thought of the specimen in front of her, she motioned to me to raise my arms. I looked at her again, but there was no response, only the feeling of her hands upon my body.

A sense of desolation developed on top of my fear, and panic-stricken thoughts raced through my mind. What if the security people decided to throw me in gaol? Who was there to care about what happened to me and who would help me? From nowhere, another thought hurtled into my mind. I thought of Brian Keenan's book, *An Evil Cradling,* about his time as a prisoner of Arab terrorists. A phrase came to me, "Whatever you do, don't show fear!" It shouted at me repeatedly until I acted on it. I withdrew my fearful gaze from the Arab woman's face and planted it straight past her on the opposite wall and then I stood erect. Those two actions put me back in control.

I nearly lost it again when I realised that her search was offensive. It was not the search that I had undergone several times at British airports when the security people frisked me. This was a grope, almost sexual in nature and designed to establish her control over me. Her hands groped firmly around my back and buttocks, under my arms and touching my breasts, down my cleavage, round my thighs and well between my legs. Instinct told me to submit – if I resisted the consequences would be much more serious. When she was finished and had found nothing, I felt her disappointment. Oozing silent resentment, she turned her back on me, marched to the door and held it open, looking straight through me again. I did the same to her as I sailed out.

In the corridor I almost threw up. I hurried through the double doors and back to the queue. Andy had waited for me and I was so glad to see his familiar face, even though I had only met him eight hours previously. He looked at me questioningly as we walked along the gangway to the aircraft. What had caused the sirens to go off had been a credit card in my neck purse and 40 rolls of film in a box in my rucksack. The fear dissolved during the rest of the flight, but it took three days for the sick feeling in my gut to go away.

Kathmandu provoked fears of a different kind. As we left the airport building to walk to our hotel minibus, we were surrounded by a swarm of children clamouring to be our guide or to carry our bags or just begging. There were about 20 of them and their noise and closeness put me on edge for fear of losing my neck purse and the camera in my small rucksack. Then an old man came towards us with pleading eyes, his body so thin that his ribs protruded through his half covered chest. I turned my back on all of it and climbed aboard the bus.

The bus itself was peaceful but the ten miles of highway into the city were like the cross-country course at the Badminton horse trials. The driver had to do much swerving and braking to avoid other vehicles, people and the sacred cows that meandered at will on the roadway. The noise level from the constant horn honking rose even higher as we entered the city and had to compete for road space with the thousands of motorbikes powered by Chinese two-stroke engines. The open windows of the minibus, with net curtains flapping in the warm breeze, helped to keep us cool, but I had visions of a hand snaking in and grabbing my purse. I was glad to reach the peace and security of my hotel room, but even there I could still smell the exhaust from the city's traffic.

That evening at dinner I started to take note of the five other trekkers. The youngest was a good-looking young man called Greg Hoggett.

Thick, dark, wavy hair crowned a kindly, open face. He and I had at least one thing in common – we were both travelling alone within the group. Phil and Eleanor sat across the table from me and next to them were Colin and Jill, a middle-aged married couple from Gloucestershire. Andy, the guide, had receding dark hair and a quick, friendly smile. His colleague, Micky Fox, was thirty-ish and quiet. He was on the trek to gain experience so that he could lead future treks. He spoke mainly to Andy. I wondered if any of the others had the same fears as me. They didn't seem to, but then no one raised the subject.

Next morning we visited the Buddhist monument at Swayambu with the all seeing eyes of the Buddha painted on the white dome. Then the minibus took us to Bhaktapur, a smaller city to the east of Kathmandu, where we were pestered again by beggars as we strolled around another monument. Each time I gave a firm "No, thank you!" they would retreat, looking at me warily.

The afternoon was spent finalising arrangements for the start of the trek the next day. Andy went to the airport to bribe a customs official to release several blue plastic barrels, one of which contained medical supplies while the others were filled with food from a Sainsburys store in Sheffield. When he returned he took me to the Thamel area of Kathmandu to hire a duvet and plastic snow boots for the trek. There were numerous shops with equipment to hire that had been left behind by previous expeditions.

An alarm call at 4.30 am on Monday 2 May roused me from a deep sleep and an hour later the minibus carried us to the airport for the early morning flight to Lukla, the airstrip for Mount Everest. An inner glow transformed any residual fear in my gut into intense excitement. Security checks at the airport were effective but relaxed – the Nepali woman burst out laughing at the toy panda in the top of my rucksack. Then we boarded the Twin Otter aircraft for our flight to Mount Everest.

The cockpit had no door and I could see the pilot apply full throttle. The sense of being close to the action and the loud whine of the engines blasted away any feelings of apprehension I had about being in a small machine passing through deep narrow valleys as we sought the Lukla landing strip. Several passengers on the aircraft pretended to be asleep to avoid looking out the window. Eleanor was pale and tense as she faced her fear of flying. I admired her courage.

Then the pilot turned the aircraft into the side valley for Lukla and everyone was silent. Lukla was a one-shot runway carved into the side of the mountain. If the pilot got it wrong, there was no possibility of going around because of the great rock wall just beyond the end of the runway. Turning back in the narrow valley would have been equally awkward. I watched the runway coming closer through the window and, as the tension mounted, I could feel laughter bubbling up.

Of course, the pilot landed us successfully, and loud chatter broke out as he taxied up the bumpy runway to the turning area at the top. Even Eleanor was smiling. We were here and even if we hadn't managed to see Mount Everest, we knew it wasn't far away.

The Hinku Valley

Our route to Mera Peak started at Lukla, at 9,000 feet above sea level. It would follow a rising trail up to the 16,217 feet Zatrwa La pass before descending into the Hinku Valley, at the bottom of which flowed the Hinku river. It had its source in the Mera Glacier, on the slopes of Mera Peak, and we would follow its course to the mountain, up on to the glacier and make High Camp at 19,000 feet. From there, we would make our attempt on the summit.

We started walking from Lukla several hours after our arrival. By then, the 23 porters and cook crew had sorted their loads while the rest of us explored Lukla. Most of the narrow streets had hard-packed mud surfaces. Construction work was going on everywhere – more prosperous buildings, usually two or three storeys, were made of stone, while the rest were made of wood. There were no cars and the air was clean. The only sounds I could hear were workmen's voices, the banging of hammers and the scraping of saws. It was a short walking day – three and a half hours to our first campsite at Chutanga. The rocky trail went uphill from Lukla and through a dense rhododendron wood to a campsite in a clearing. We were now at 10,000 feet.

I made a poor beginning at Chutanga. I was tired and hungry – lunch had consisted of a half-cooked pizza in a lodging house near the airstrip – and it had started to rain. When Andy had finished helping me pitch my tent, I crawled in and found that it leaked. And my luggage hadn't arrived. I swore to myself about the conditions and then I heard Cyril's strong Sheffield voice in my ear: "Stop mithering!

You have this to put up with so get on with it!" So I did, and a dinner of vegetable soup and hot stew cheered me enormously. I'm not at my best when hungry.

Next morning I woke at 5 am to 'bed-tea' brought by smiling Sherpas. Then I came out of my tent but soon went back for my camera. Numbur Peak, a mountain of 22,818 feet, raised its huge, glacier-covered face across the valley beyond the rhododendron trees. Its gleaming ridges stood starkly against bright blue sky. This was why I'd come to Nepal.

Andy declared a rest day. After a breakfast of porridge and eggs, we strolled up the wooded trail for an hour. We had a short rest and returned to camp. The idea was to help the acclimatisation process so that when we set off up the trail the next day, we would already have made inroads into that day's altitude gain. We dined again in the early evening and I went to bed at 8 pm. This became a pattern, as did the early morning starts.

On the third day I reached the Zatrwa La in the company of Colin and Jill who were a united couple, reserved and quiet. It was the Sherpas who brightened up my morning. As we contoured around the shoulder of the pass, three of them, heavily laden, went running past on an uphill section of trail, singing a lively song. Amazed, I watched as they disappeared around a rock corner. When I reached the spot I was greatly relieved to find them collapsed on the ground, loads abandoned and one of them dragging on a cigarette. I caught the smoker's eye and we started to laugh. It was an example of the Sherpas' delightful sense of humour and their way of showing us who was really in charge on the mountain. We might have the money, but we were novices in their environment.

We descended a long, rocky trail into the Hinku Valley through open terrain. I travel better where I can see the way ahead, rather than being enclosed in woodland. That night, our route along the valley firmly established, we camped at Tashing Ongma. I sat on the ground in my tent, writing my journal, as the Sherpas cooked dinner in the cook tent, singing softly and melodically as they worked. It was a moment of musical munificence.

En route to Ghotse the next day we had our first sight of Mera Peak. We came around a corner on the trail and there it was. Twelve miles away and 8,000 feet higher than where we stood, its huge west face rose majestically to glacier-covered triple summits; the middle peak would be our target on summit day. For several minutes I gazed at it, hardly able to take it in that, weather and health permitting, we would be standing there in a few days' time. Before we walked on I named the flat, rounded summit the 'Christmas Cake' because that was what it looked like.

The descent to Ghotse was through another rhododendron wood with obstructive tree roots and rocks. The constant change of surface was merciless on my feet and the bunion at the base of my left big toe objected loudly to this treatment. Nevertheless, as I slipped into sleep that night, I had a deep sense of peace and contentment. Dubai security was far away.

Next day, on the trail to Tangnag, the contentment and ease persisted. I found myself walking alone, having lost contact with Andy and Greg, and I enjoyed the restful solitude of good mountain walking.

The sun was shining, the birds singing, the river was roaring along its course and the mountains were clear and high in every direction.

An hour later I entered the small summer settlement of Tangnag with Andy whom I'd caught up. Several long, low, bamboo matting huts were surrounded by small potato fields. Andy persuaded a Sherpani in the last hut to make tea for us and a young boy, dark haired and bright-eyed, invited me in to sit on a mattress near the fire. Wooden frames supported shelves filled with pots and pans made of Indian steel, bottles of Nepali rum and tins of food. Outside, it started to rain and a woman came into the hut dragging two sheets of white plastic filled with potatoes which she had been sorting. I also met my first yak in Tangnag. The big-horned, hairy animal was snuffling along the dry stone wall surrounding our camping field. I kept out of its way and Andy said, "Good move. They're very bad tempered – don't get in their way or they will simply stab you!" I learned that yak can only live above 10,000 feet and they carry two porter loads.

The last day in the Hinku Valley was hard. We turned east along the head of the valley to our base camp which was to be established at Khare, at 16,400 feet, but as soon as I left Tangnag I was in trouble. For the first time I was seriously affected by altitude. I couldn't eat breakfast because I felt nauseous and the queasiness stayed with me as I walked. My energy evaporated and my legs felt heavy. I dragged my feet as, slowly, I gained height, and hardly had the energy to lift them over the rocks on the trail. After several hours I reached Khare and when the Sherpas spread out a groundsheet, I lay down on it. In seconds, I was asleep and didn't move even when hailstones fell on me and a cold wind blew across the camp ground. Andy and Greg put my tent up and I climbed into my sleeping bag. Apart from waking up for the drinks that the Sherpas brought me, I slept for 18 hours and happily, when I woke the following morning, I was fully recovered.

Altitude sickness is insidious – it creeps up on you but its cumulative effects can soon create a crisis. It is caused by lack of oxygen in the air, which affects the blood's ability to carry fluids around the body; fluid then gathers on the lungs which makes breathing difficult. The problem is dealt with by the regular use of water tablets and gaining height gradually. The rest day that Andy declared at Khare was a vital opportunity for everyone to acclimatise. To prepare for the ascent to High Camp on the Mera Glacier, he persuaded us to take our ice axes, plastic boots and crampons to the foot of the glacier. I arrived there with him and Greg and the three of us practised using crampons and moving roped up. Greg clearly knew what he was doing, while I kept checking my crampon straps – I hated the feeling that they might come off my boots at a vital moment. We left our equipment under a rock and strolled back to Khare.

Sitting in my tent before dinner, I reflected on the last six days on trek. Overall, I was happy on the journey. Only on the first day, at Chutanga, had I been seriously lonely for Cyril; the rest of the time I was too preoccupied with the physical challenge of the journey and social challenge of the new company in which I found myself. I seemed to get on best with Andy and Greg, and socialised with the others at meal times. But however well I related to my companions, the void left by Cyril's death was always there, waiting for me to fall into it.

Tension mounted in Base Camp. Summit day was only two days away and in the morning we would be starting the long pull up on to the glacier. As we took our seats at the dinner table in the mess tent that night, I looked round at our party. Phil and Eleanor were full of the challenge to come; Micky was strangely quiet; Colin and Jill sat with eyes unusually bright; Greg laughed his way through the meal; and I kept smiling. Then, as the dirty plates were cleared away, Andy cut through the excitement like a whip. In a lull in the conversation, he said, "Tonight we have to make some hard decisions." There was silence. He went on, "Some of us have been suffering from altitude sickness and won't be able to go for the summit. I want you to make your own decisions."

The mess tent cleared rapidly, with a few murmured "Good nights." I followed the others out into the darkening campsite and the communal anxiety was tangible even in the open air. I could hear the same question in everyone's mind: "Is it me?" Each of us had suffered from early symptoms of altitude sickness. Stumbling to my tent, all I could think about was whether I would lose my mountain. As I crawled on my knees through the door I thought of my fatigue and nausea of the day before. Did Andy mean me? I hadn't noticed anyone else having problems, mainly because I either walked on my own or with Greg, and he seemed to cope well with everything. What was I to do? For a moment I thought of Phil, Eleanor, Colin and Jill. I'd watched them go quietly to their tents and envied their togetherness. I was dealing with this alone and my mind whirled in search of an answer.

Suddenly, I needed a toilet. Back out in the cold and gloom, my eyes scanned the campsite. There was a shortage of toilet facilities at Khare, mainly because what wasn't rock was frozen ground. It hadn't been possible for the Sherpas to dig a latrine and put a tent over it. I spotted a large boulder, the size of a small house, about 100 yards from my tent. I walked across to it, looking round for lurking Sherpas who seemed to have a compulsive curiosity about western toilet habits. As I came round to the 'private' side of the rock, I found the toilet was a shit bed. The whole area was littered with small piles of human faeces decorated with pieces of pink toilet paper. The sight seemed to emphasise the awfulness of my mountain dilemma, but I had to face them both. Misery filled me as I found a spot for myself right on the edge of the area. Squatting, I started to weep. I had never felt so desolate – I was alone in a shit bed, and I was going to lose my mountain. My tears flowed and, in the midst of all that misery and shit, I bawled for Cyril. And I got my answer.

Everything went still and quiet. I waited. Cyril answered. I heard a voice inside my head, clear as day: "Dyson, you can do this. You've been here before, not in this physical place, but you've had to make hard, lonely decisions before. You can do this!" Having completed my contribution to the communal toilet, I walked calmly back to my tent. All tears were gone.

Mera Peak

I'd talked to Cyril every day since he died, usually to a photograph of him, which I had placed on the coffee table in front of my lounge window. I'd stand in front of it and tell him what was on my mind and ask for any help I needed. I love that photograph. It was taken at a friend's wedding near Selby in North Yorkshire. Following the early afternoon ceremony in a village church, we had waited almost an hour while the photographer took pictures of everything, even the plant pots in the church porch. Impatient and hungry for our dinner, we left and drove to the hotel where the reception was being held. When we arrived, we found the staff rather tense as the wedding party was already late and the bar was shut. All we could do was sit and wait, and that was when the photograph was taken. Cyril is sitting in the bar with his elbows resting on a table and holding his pipe on which he had drawn. The look in his eyes is one of contentment, of a man happy in his world. I was the reason for that look: if I've done nothing else right in my life, I've done that.

Desire to test myself for the physical challenge of Mera Peak forced me out of my sleeping bag at 4.30 am. I was ready to leave an hour later and the only person ahead of me out of the camp was Andy. I almost caught him up on the trail, but he kept pulling away from me and I was 5 minutes behind him when I reached the foot of the glacier. He gave me a strange look as I arrived and said, "Well, I'm surprised it's you, but you're here and you're on the first rope!" It didn't sink in at first, but then I realised I was on the A team and he had made no mention of altitude sickness. I thanked Cyril for the miracle.

Colin and Greg arrived soon afterwards and the four of us would make the first rope. Andy was leader, Greg followed him, then myself, and Colin brought up the rear. I learned from Andy that it was Jill who had been suffering from severe symptoms of altitude sickness and had to make a painful decision. The second rope was led by Micky, followed by Phil, then Eleanor and Lakpa Nuru, a climbing Sherpa.

Andy briefed us on the glacier before we set off: "Keep the rope stretched out between you. Then, if someone does go into a crevasse, they won't go far. Besides, the crevasses are generally narrow and your rucksack will usually stop you going in any further than your waist. This is a safe glacier without too many crevasses, but you can't take the chance. So be ready to jump back if the person ahead slips down. Get your ice axe in!"

Roped and cramponed, we set off up the glacier towards the Mera La which was at 17,767 feet. The soft snow made the going strenuous. Once we had reached the almost unnoticeable pass, the glacier sloped upwards in a south-westerly direction towards the summit. Andy kept testing the ground ahead for crevasses by poking it with his ice axe. All I thought about was putting one foot in front of the other and I put the notion of falling into a crevasse out of my mind. If anyone was going to fall in one, it would be Andy …

"Jesus, shit!"

Suddenly I was in one. I yelled out in instant fright, partly convinced that I was going to slither hundreds of feet to my death and partly convinced that the rope would save me. Breathing hard, I swung my ice axe into the surface of the glacier and was slow to realise that, if I could do so, I couldn't have fallen very far at all; but you don't think that at the time. Still terrified of a long drop, I flailed my legs around as I tried to dig the toe points of my crampons into the side of the crevasse. Then I felt a pull on the rope and it was Greg, urging me forward over the edge of the crevasse into which I'd only fallen up to my waist. As Andy had predicted, my rucksack had effectively blocked me from going more than a few feet into the narrow entrance of the crevasse. Moments later I had wriggled my way on to the surface and stumbled to my feet and, not for the first time on this journey, I was grateful to Greg.

His hallmark was his kindness. I'd walked with him for part of each day since the beginning of the trek and come to know something about him. He was 23, mountain fit and had climbed in Scotland. Yet he still found time to go hill walking with his mother. I was probably about the same age as her and, whether or not he recognised something of her in me, he showed me a rare courtesy and kindness. Among other things, he had helped Andy erect my tent the day I suffered from altitude sickness. Most 23-year-olds would have little patience with slower moving older women.

Four hours after we left Khare we reached the site of High Camp. It was located near a large outcrop of black rocks, the only substantial landmark on the expanse of glacier. Andy carefully checked the site for crevasses and once it was declared safe, the Sherpas pitched our tents in a row. While they were busy, I made a full scan of the surrounding mountains and the efforts of the last nine days were rewarded. To the south-east rose a massive mountain, whose black rocky ramparts were supported by sharp ridges that led upwards to a pronounced pyramidal summit. "That's Makalu," Andy told me, "it's the sixth highest mountain in the world." Closer to Mera Peak was Chamlang, its pyramid-shaped face covered with snow and ice. I seemed to be finding pyramids everywhere. Andy sent us all to bed at 1 pm.

For the rest of the day he organised the Sherpas to bring us juice, tea, soup and spaghetti bolognaise. The drinks were to ensure that we were well hydrated and the spaghetti was to load us with carbohydrates for the effort to come, but by the time I'd had three helpings, I was heartily sick of it. Summit day started with bed-tea at 11.30 pm. The ascent was to be made in the dark so that, at the end of a long day, when exhaustion could lead to mistakes, there would be a wide safety margin of daylight.

After two hours of intense activity around the camp while everyone sorted their gear, we assembled in our 'ropes' of four. There was yet another change of personnel. Micky, who had made it to High Camp, decided to abandon his attempt on the summit as he had been seriously affected by altitude. The second rope was now led by Lakpa Nuru, followed by Phil, then Eleanor, with a climbing Sherpa called Temba bringing up the rear. Andy's rope set off first, the broad beams from our head torches showing the ground ahead, which Andy continuously tested for crevasses. It was Wednesday 11 May 1994.

It was a long ascent of slow, steady plodding, which is the best way at altitude. We stopped frequently for short rests and, while my overworked lungs and fast-beating heart came back to a tolerable state,

I looked up at the night sky. It was a fabulous sight. The velvety black of the sky sparkled and glinted with the stars of the Milky Way, which looked very different here from how it looked over Sheffield. We were directly under a broad band of densely starred sky and it was as though we had opened a universal crate of high quality diamonds. In the deepest part of the night, Greg suddenly cried, "Look at that!" To the north, we saw great flashes of coloured light passing over the outline of high mountains – an electrical storm. Flash followed flash of green, pink, yellow, blue and white. I shivered as I watched it: the temperature had dropped to –10 degrees Celsius. I put on my down jacket.

The first sign of sunrise was a hint of light behind the peaks on the eastern horizon. When the sun did finally rise, it threw a golden light across the Himalayas, which bounced off the gleaming snow. At 7.30 am, six hours after we started out, we reached the base of the 'Christmas Cake', the central summit of Mera Peak.

Exhausted, we stood looking up at the last 100 feet of snow that separated us from our goal. To our dismay, it was wet and soft and contained an evil-looking crevasse 15 feet above us. This was where Andy earned his salary. A short conference with Lakpa Nuru resulted in the Sherpa attaching a rope to his waist belt, adjusting his snow goggles and then, with remarkable agility, almost sprinting up the steep, wet snow until he disappeared over the top. Five minutes later, his smiling face reappeared and, in his hand, he waved the end of a rope which he sent snaking down to us. Andy turned to us and said lightly, "We're going to climb the rope. Have you jumared before?"

Jumaring is a technique for climbing a rope. A jumar is a D-shaped piece of metal which is attached to the rope with a friction nut. When the nut is released with a small lever, the climber can slide the jumar up the rope and then let the friction nut tighten again. The other main feature is a hole in the metal through which a loop of rope can be passed and attached to the climber's harness or belt. That keeps the climber secured to the jumar which is, of course, secured to the rope.

At 21,100 feet in the Himalayas I learned to jumar. It was the steepest learning curve I have ever experienced but at that point, I was aware that nothing was going to stop me standing on the summit, short of dropping dead. Greg went before me and disappeared over the edge of the Christmas Cake. Then it was my turn.

Andy climbed up alongside me for the first 20 feet and I soon realised that there was some purchase for my feet in the wet snow. That allowed me moments in which I could move the jumar up the rope and, then, supported by it, I could find a new foothold. The 100 feet seemed a long way but at last I reached the top. I came over the edge of the Christmas Cake on my hands and knees, gasping for breath in the cold wind. Lakpa gave me a helpful tug on the rope and Greg came forward to help me to my feet. Straight ahead was what I'd waited 25 years to see.

Central to the view was the pyramid summit of Mount Everest, 29,029 feet high, with its customary wisp of white cloud blowing over its eastern shoulder. Further east, next to it, was the huge, black, south face of Lhotse, at 27,890 feet the fourth highest mountain in the world; extending away from that was a serrated, snowy ridge leading to the pale rock face of Baruntse. To the west of Everest was Nuptse, a long, black, rocky ridge of mountain, at 25,905 feet. I stared and stared.

As I looked, Lakpa released me from the jumar. I withdrew from the others and gazed at my heart's desire. To the south-east of Everest, Makalu and Chamlang showed up against the burning blue sky, their perspective now so altered that I was able to look down on the deep valleys and slender ridges that filled the space between them and Mera Peak. I scanned the whole horizon. Over to the east, rising out of a thick layer of white cloud, was the extended shape of Kangchenjunga, at 28,802 feet the third highest mountain in the world. My eyes were drawn inexorably back to Everest. I felt a growing blockage in my throat.

When the thought of Cyril came to me, I started sobbing and couldn't stop. In my heart I thanked him for getting me there, and an unexpected voice inside me said, "This is for you; I give this mountain to you." Then I did what I'd made up my mind to do if I reached the summit of Mera Peak.

My ice axe was stuck in the ground on the Everest side of the summit. While the others gathered near Lakpa waiting for Phil to arrive, I stood near the axe facing Mount Everest. I raised my arms and at the top of my voice I bellowed across the Himalayas:
"CYRIL!"

The mountain was his.

The Amphu Lupsta

We stayed on the summit for 30 minutes to savour the achievement. The strengthening wind blew the prayer flags off their bamboo poles and the lowering temperature caused me to pull my down jacket tight around me. When it was time to go, I said a silent, happy "Goodbye" to Everest and climbed down the wet snow on a tight rope held by Lakpa, who seemed immune to the cold. When I joined the others at the foot of the Christmas Cake, my jaws ached from endless smiling.

The descent to High Camp took four hours. My legs were heavy with exhaustion and I struggled to keep up with Andy and Greg but, once we had passed the camp, Andy slowed the pace down to suit me. On the last stretch of rocky trail to our new campsite, in a small side valley off the Upper Hongu, we unroped and the others went on ahead. I plodded slowly after them, stopping every few minutes to sit and rest. The trail ended 50 yards from the camp and Jill came to meet me. "You did it!" she said. I could hear the ache in her voice as she went on, "I wish I could have gone, but I just don't feel well." I muttered something about her health being more important than the summit, but it was small consolation.

That night I slept for 13 hours and woke to the luxury of a Himalayan 'lie-in' – bed-tea didn't arrive until 7 am. A leisurely breakfast was followed by a mid-morning departure for the short walk to our next campsite – the Chamlang Base Camp, from which expeditions to that mountain set out. It was a flat, rocky area where it was hard to get tent pegs into the ground. While the Sherpas struggled with that, Andy advised us to walk further up the valley. Greg and I did so, following the faint trail northwards and, passing the end of a low moraine, we had a magical and uninterrupted view of Everest and Lhotse.

The rest of the day was spent relaxing in camp. It was a time for reflection and journal writing. I thought about the intense emotions of the day before on Mera Peak. Everyone in the summit party had been moved – the women shed tears and the men went quiet. I thought about my feeling that Cyril was nearby as I stood looking at Everest and how I had given my mountain to him. It was clear to me that he would always be a part of my life and not just in memories: I had a sense of him being in every cell of my body – it was as though his 'mesh' was merged with mine. I had rich memories, but I also believed I had more. Cyril's influence and presence had become part of my 'blue-print', the entire physical, emotional, intellectual and spiritual package that was Sheila Dyson.

The successful ascent of Mera Peak had a positive effect on everyone, including the climbing Sherpas. While we lazed about the camp that morning, they lay on their stomachs in a row in the sunshine. They were physically nearer to us than they had been all trek, when at night they had preferred to sleep in nearby caves rather than in the tents provided. Now they came close to us, as though drawn by the smell of success. Andy said, "They're pleased with themselves and us. When they go home, they'll have greater status in their own villages and they'll be employed again as porters and climbing Sherpas. In fact, Lakpa has been to the summit of Everest." I looked across at Lakpa, lying on the end of the row of Sherpas. He still wore his snow goggles of the day before, even though there was no snow where we were. He was probably enjoying his moment of glory as, without him, our arrival at the summit of Mera Peak would have been much more difficult.

Greg took a photograph of me with two Sherpanis, of whom there were three among the cook crew. My skin colour now matched theirs. I had been surprised that there were any women among the porters and cook crew, and it struck me that these young Buddhist women had a real chance of paid employment. Life seemed to hold more possibilities for them than the Hindu women of lower caste who, I learned, in remote areas were regarded as chattels by their fathers and husbands and could be given in marriage for the price of a buffalo.

The following day, two days after Mera Peak, we walked almost the full length of the Hongu Valley to our new campsite at Panch Pokhari. It was close to the 18,963 feet Amphu Lapsta pass, over which we would travel down into a side valley off the Everest Base Camp trail. This was in the centre of the Khumbu region, the traditional home of the Sherpas.

I struggled all day. Every 30 yards or so along the trail, I had to stop while I caught my breath. We passed several semi-frozen lakes, called *pokhari* in Sherpa. Much of the valley floor was covered by moraines and boulder fields left behind by retreating glaciers and the rock-strewn trail through the area caused massive stress on people's legs. The weather was whimsical. The sun was hot and we sweated but, if we removed any item of clothing, a stiff, cold wind caused a rapid loss of body heat. It was such a troublesome day that I couldn't even enjoy the sight of Everest ahead. When the Sherpas had pitched my tent at Panch Pokhari, I wriggled into my sleeping bag. My limbs were tired and heavy and my mouth hurt from burns and split lips from the cold air. Even the top of my tongue had been burnt by the sun and there was no comfort in talking or eating. I slept.

We had a final camp in the Hongu Valley close to the foot of the Amphu Lapsta. Andy briefed us in the mess tent that night: "Tomorrow is going to be the most technical day of the journey. We'll be going over the glacier which is full of crevasses but there is a straightforward, safe gulley. You'll have to have your wits about you. The Sherpas will be going up the same gulley on a separate rope. And another thing, when you get to the top, don't go running ahead. It's very narrow and you'll go clean over the other side. It's a long way down!" The atmosphere was tense as we said goodnight.

The morning came crisp and clear and a short walk past several moraines brought us to the edge of the glacier. Jill, once again troubled by altitude sickness, looked miserable as she stood waiting for us to rope up. I was glad to be on a similar rope to summit day – Andy led, followed by Greg, then myself, with Eleanor bringing up the rear. The more I saw of Eleanor, the more I admired her. She was scared of heights and scared of flying. She cried when Phil disappeared into a crevasse on the Mera Glacier and was deeply relieved when the Sherpas pulled him out on the rope. Yet she had chosen to come to Nepal and, despite her fears, was clearly enjoying the mountains. The Amphu Lapsta was exciting, from our first steps on the steep glacier, through our passage up the crowded gulley, to our arrival on the

*Cyril and Sheila,
wedding day in Sheffield,
2 August 1984*

Photo: R. Davis

*Cyril and Sheila on
Mount Parnassus in
Greece, May 1990*

Mum at her back door in Sheffield　　　　　*Photo: S. Dyson*

Aerial view of Stanage Edge, Derbyshire, taken from G-AJIT　　　　*Photo: S. Cullen*

Sheila on the summit of Mera Peak, 21,247 feet, 12 miles from Mount Everest in the background

Photo: G. Hoggett

Sheila on the top of the Amphu Lapsta, 18,963 feet, seven miles from Everest in background

Photo: G. Hoggett

Namgey and Bhutia outside Namgey Hotel, Taplejung

Photo: S. Dyson

Kasang and Temba in the dining room of Namgey Hotel, Taplejung

Photo: S. Dyson

exposed, narrow spot that was the top of the pass. It was also the finest mountaineering day of my life.

As we progressed up the glacier to the bottom of the gulley, I moved with a growing confidence. I found it hard to believe that doing something this challenging, I could feel so good. Once in the gulley, Andy organised our group. Lakpa had already put in place a fixed rope to help the porters carry their heavy loads up the steep snow. They clipped on to the rope which served as a kind of bannister. I watched them as they moved up, their bodies almost hidden under huge loads. We were to climb alongside them.

Andy went up first, belayed himself at the top and threw a rope down to us. Greg followed. As I waited, two porters struggled past our narrow spot. Once they were gone, I had a clear view of the hanging glacier that goes right up and over the pass. It was in decay and deep, wide crevasses had opened with no visible bottoms. Sections of it took the form of ice towers, precariously holding on to the main body of the glacier, but just waiting to collapse and avalanche down into the Hongu Valley. Inside the crevasses, I could see layer upon layer of snow and ice, each representing a year's snowfall.

Soon it was my turn to climb the gulley. I tied on to the rope and started up the snow. I loved it. The snow was firm and good and my ice axe and crampons had something to dig into. I passed two porters going up and took care not to get in their way. When I reached the top, I grinned at Andy and he grinned back.

He motioned me to pass him and continue on out of the gulley to the top of the pass itself. Still roped, I suddenly reached the highest point.

I stopped dead – there was nowhere else to go except over the other side. Right in front of me, seeming so close that I could almost touch it with my hand, was the great south face of Lhotse, the fourth highest mountain in the world. Hiding behind its shoulder, was the pyramid summit of Everest, a mere seven miles away and 10,000 feet above me. This was better than Mera Peak – here I was so much closer and the dramatic nearness of these magnificent mountains was almost unbearable. I didn't cry on top of the Amphu Lapsta – instead, I was unable to stop grinning like an idiot. I knew Cyril would have been satisfied with my performance: it had been a neat bit of mountaineering.

When I managed to tear my eyes off Lhotse and Everest, I saw that the rocky ground on which we stood looked like piles of broken slate, and close by were broken lumps of creamy quartzite. Andy appeared on the top of the pass to organise our descent down into the side valley off the Khumbu. The climbing Sherpas had placed a fixed rope on the descent route and we clipped on to it. Colin had joined us and Andy arranged that the three of us would descend together. Colin went first, followed by me and Greg. We stepped over a small crevasse and Andy watched as I descended over some difficult mixed ground of rock and snow. He gave me a curious look and said, "You've found your niche in life!"

Down the fixed rope I went, following as it snaked along several snow ramps. There was another challenge ahead in the form of a steep rock band. Andy stood there next to Dawa Temba, the sirdar, who was belayed at the top of it. Andy said, "You can abseil down if you want, or climb down, or Dawa can lower you down. It's your choice!" None of these methods of descent held much appeal. Abseiling terrified me and being lowered down would put me in a position of complete dependence on the person holding the rope. So I elected to climb down, but on a tight rope to give me security and control over the 1,000 feet drop to the rocky valley below. My only concern as I tied on to Dawa's rope was whether he would understand my cries for help if I came off the rock.

There were solid hand and footholds for the first 20 feet and Dawa let the rope out slowly so it remained taut. Then the rock face changed and there were fewer holds. I could find only small, sloping ledges and became ever more mindful of the space beneath me. My grip on the rock face became tenuous and my knees started to tremble. It was only a matter of time – "Tight rope!" I yelled at Dawa and I was gone. I screamed as hands and feet slid away from the rock. Dawa may not have understood my English swearing but he certainly understood my tone. The rope jerked tight and I was held, dangling in space and swinging gently as, with mad energy, my hands and feet scrabbled over the rock face, desperately searching for holds. Somehow I found them and gripped on hard. I glanced up to see Dawa, his hands firmly in place on the mechanism controlling the run of the rope and a huge grin on his face. He was laughing at me!

Once past the rock band, we crossed several sloping snowfields, interspersed with areas of broken rock. The descent to the valley floor had taken several hours and, as we reached the lower ground, we faced only rough moraines and boulder fields. I turned back to look at the

3,000 feet wall we had come down. Even I was impressed with myself. On we went. At last we came over the final moraine of the day to a flat area next to the Imja Khola river which meandered down the valley. As I walked into the lunch spot, I saw that the cook crew had set up a stove with a big pot of soup on top. Feeling thirsty and exhausted, I said in a weak voice, just like they do in the movies, "Water, water!" and everyone, including the Sherpas, laughed at me. Later, I had three bowls of soup for lunch.

After that I dropped to the back of the line. I'd made my big effort on the Amphu Lapsta and now I took to ambling along, content to let the day go by. Andy arranged for Lakpa to be the 'sweeper' of our group and he escorted me for the rest of the day's walk. He even carried my day sack for me, perhaps in the vain hope that I might get to camp sooner. I kept looking sideways at him as I'd never had the exclusive company of someone who had done the 'Big One'.

Lakpa was a small, wiry man with a face burnished by the sun, although he had a patch of light skin on his left cheek. Having watched him perform on rock and ice for several days, I knew he had the extraordinary wiry strength and endurance of the climbing Sherpas. His limited English was spoken with a strong Sherpa accent and I found it hard to hear what he said. Unfortunately for him, I had no Sherpa. Despite this unpromising beginning, we talked all the way to our new campsite at Chhukung. We spoke of the flowers, the birds and the surrounding mountains. He told me he had two children, including a son born only two months before of whom he was inordinately proud. I tried to tell him something about life in England.

At Chhukung I bought him a bottle of San Miguel beer in a summerhouse made of bamboo matting. When I presented it to him, he looked at me solemnly, poured it into a glass and sat at the hearth drinking it slowly. He took a long poker and urged the wooden embers into flame. I had a feeling that this was what he would be like at home – a Sherpa in charge of his own hearth.

We camped in a field near the summer settlement and, as I lay in my tent resting before dinner, I thought what an enjoyable day it had been. All day I had felt positive and capable, despite my moment on the rock band. To me, that was normal fear, different in nature from that generated by Dubai security, and I had been able to overcome it and laugh about it. Without any of their language, I was also able to laugh with the Sherpas. It was a time of uplift rare for me in the long period of dreariness since Cyril's death. After dinner, I turned in early. The porters had settled in a house near our camp, no doubt belonging to their relatives, and I could hear them singing before they went to sleep. I loved to hear them sing – they had a soft, rounded tone and a steady, easy rhythm. The harmony of men and mountains was complete and I slept.

The Lonely Khumbu

From Chukung we travelled westwards to Dingboche, our first permanent settlement for 12 days. High up on the hillside an elaborate chorten, or wayside shrine, emphasised the importance of the village. A string of prayer flags attached to the chorten blew in the wind as the dark clouds of late morning blotted out the surrounding mountains. It started to rain just as we entered a lodging house for a lunchtime San Miguel. We camped that night in a field near the village centre.

Beyond Dingboche the trail reached a junction with the Everest Base Camp trail which we followed next day to Pangboche, a sizeable permanent settlement where some of our Sherpas had relatives. We were now in the heart of the Khumbu, the traditional home of the Sherpas, who are Buddhist and who were originally a nomadic race from Tibet. To celebrate their homecoming, the resident Sherpas threw a party for our Sherpas and we were all invited. Feeling too tired, I didn't go, but I might as well have done. At 10 pm the party was in full swing with the Sherpas singing the same short-versed song over and over again and dancing on the floorboards as though they were trying to beat them to death. In between the bursts of song, there were exuberant whoops and yells and it was impossible not to be struck by the sheer joy reverberating through the settlement and shaking the walls of my tent. At midnight all went quiet and I eventually slept but next morning the cook crew were unusually subdued. Our breakfast was late and badly cooked.

That day we walked to a place I was longing to see – Namche Bazaar, the Sherpa capital of the Khumbu. Its name features regularly in the mountaineering history of the region and, to me, it has a mystical quality. En route we would visit another village with an evocative name, Thyangboche, where there is a monastery to which members of Everest expeditions go to get the blessing of the lama.

Thyangboche disappointed me – the clouds blocked out the view of Everest and the monastery was shut. As we neared Namche, we started to meet trekkers and tourists, mainly Indian and American. Fortunately, Namche Bazaar itself is too remote to suffer from tourist sleaze.

Our resting place for the next two days was Himalayan Lodge, a substantial, three-storey stone building close to the centre of town. My room was over the front door. The prospect of a bed, albeit a simple wooden frame with a foam mattress, was appealing. I dropped my luggage and joined the others in the dining room where I indulged a recent fantasy – beer and chips. After days of eating dried and packet trekking food, it was a glorious indulgence to drink several bottles of beer and plough my way through a large plate of Sherpa stew and a big bowl of chips. We passed the afternoon in luxurious idleness – there was to be no more walking for two days. We chatted, played cards and drank beer. Then we had our evening meal with yet more chips and beer. The beer was a mistake.

Soon after the meal, I started feeling drunk. I'd forgotten about the exaggerated effects of alcohol at altitude and Namche is at 11,000 feet. Head spinning, I decided to turn in. I bade the others a groggy "Goodnight" and proceeded in an unsteady manner up the wooden stairs. The extra 10 feet of altitude seemed to affect me. I turned down the corridor towards my room and saw a young man trying the door. I shouted at him, "What are you doing at my room?" I didn't wait for his answer but shouted again, "Leave my things alone!" He made a rapid movement and was gone. I stood swaying in the corridor, my mouth flapping open a couple of times before I dizzied the short distance to my room and fell in the door. After that, I knew nothing until I woke up cold and shivering in the early hours covered only by my cagoule. With head spinning, I pulled my sleeping bag from my big rucksack and somehow wound my way into it on top of the foam mattress.

At 6 am I came to, feeling as though I had banged my head repeatedly against the wooden wall. My stomach sent up waves of rebellious nausea. My left ear felt sore and when I touched it, it bled. Then I noticed a large, deep bruise on my left thigh. What had I been up to? Opening my eyes a little more I glanced round the room, which looked a mess. My clothes were scattered everywhere. I sat up slowly and spotted my red neck purse under the bed. It was empty. Suddenly, I stood up in the middle of the mess and said in an outraged voice, "I've been robbed!" The outrage was combined with a flicker of the fear and vulnerability I had felt in Kathmandu. I looked about the room for any clues and something made me sift through the tangle of clothes and gear. I picked over a crumpled sweater and felt a ray of hope when a pile of ruppee notes fell out. I searched on and found my travellers' cheques and coins in a clump of dirty socks. I almost cried with relief.

Sitting alone, I felt distinctly embarrassed at my outburst of the previous evening. Had anyone in my group seen or heard me on the stairs or in my room? This was a real concern as the internal construction of the lodging house consisted of wooden planks for the walls, floors and ceilings, none of which lined up properly. I was able to see into the rooms on either side of mine through gaps in the wall, I could hear the Sherpas arguing in the kitchen through the gaps in the floor, and I could hear the rats scampering across the ceiling. At breakfast that morning I kept my head down and concentrated on my bowl of porridge. No one made any comments and I didn't raise the subject.

This was my last full day with my fellow travellers. I spent much of it in the company of Andy who gave me useful tips for my extended journey to the Kangchenjunga region. However, this was a journey I would be making alone, apart from the company of a Sherpa guide who would also act as translator. At home in Sheffield it had seemed an exciting thing to be taking on, but now that I had to face the reality of being alone in Nepal, it was as scary as it was exciting. I didn't stop to question if I was doing the right thing – perhaps I would have done if I knew what lay ahead of me. That afternoon I bought some cotton napkins as a present for Lakpa for his baby son – a Sherpa in a sewing shop hemmed the edges for me and wrapped the napkins in brown paper. I turned in early.

That night I woke several times, apprehensive at the imminent departure of the others. Lakpa brought bed-tea at 5.30 am and I presented him with the parcel. He took it and bowed several times as he withdrew from my room. He put it under his arm and went back to work. I said my goodbyes to Eleanor, Phil and Greg at breakfast and then walked a short distance with Colin and Jill down the Lukla trail and waved them on their way. On the way back I met Andy who wished me well and I felt the tears pricking as I said goodbye to him – I was now truly alone in Nepal and the loneliness hit me as I returned to Himalayan Lodge.

I ate a solitary lunch without any real idea of what I was going to do next. Not wanting to be conspicuously alone in the large half-empty dining room, I went out into the main street for a walk. Within five minutes I fell into conversation with another trekker called Geraldine who came from London. Standing by a souvenir stall, she told me she was going next day to Thame, a village about three hours' walk from Namche and which boasted a Buddhist monastery where there was to be a festival called Mani Rimdu. "Everyone's going," she said, referring to the other trekkers at Himalayan Lodge and, for want of something better to do, I decided to go too.

I reached Thame at lunch time next day and found lodgings in Choyo Lodge on the edge of the settlement. In the large kitchen I drank a cup of milky Sherpa tea and watched four Sherpanis getting ready for the festival up at the *gompa* or monastery. Each put on a clean shift over their silk blouses and tied a closely woven apron around their front. A shawl completed their dress and then they attended to their hair, two of them decorating their plaits with tassels. The women talked and laughed and drank endless cups of Sherpa tea. The house was quiet after they left.

The monastery was 30 minutes' walk uphill from Choyo Lodge. The main ceremony of the day was held in an inner courtyard and on the way in I bought a white silk prayer scarf. I found a seat on a low wall next to a middle-aged man from Kent. The place was teeming with Sherpas, Sherpanis and their children, and about a hundred westerners. Two monks in maroon habits blew on the long stem of big horns to produce a strong vibrant sound that was the signal for the procession of monks, young and old, to begin. The crowds moved to the edge of the courtyard which was soon filled with rows of monks and then all eyes turned to the monastery door and the Chief Lama made his dignified entrance. He took his place on the dais at the back of the courtyard, the music stopped and the blessings began.

As I joined the line of people waiting for a blessing, I could feel a rising sense of longing for human warmth. In the midst of all these strangers, I was to receive a blessing and when my turn came, I stood in front of the lama who regarded me with a tranquil air. I handed him the thin silk prayer scarf and he raised it and placed it smoothly around my neck. I had a sense of spiritual warmth and could feel the tears pricking at the back of my eyes. His gesture seemed an acknowledgement of my need.

At dinner that night in Choyo Lodge I comforted myself with beer and chips. I passed a restless night in the mixed dormitory – there were 12 of us, men and women in together – and next day I woke feeling lightheaded and dizzy and with little appetite. I decided to return to Namche, even though I would miss the main ceremonies of the festival. On the way back I passed dozens of Sherpas and Sherpanis walking up the trail. Most of them looked at me curiously: to the sociable Sherpas, being alone is almost a tragedy. The longing of the day before returned and I wept for Cyril in between meeting yet more groups of festival-bound Sherpas.

I calmed down as I descended into Namche and reached Himalayan Lodge. Anu, the owner, had kept my room for me and, as I arranged my belongings, I felt the tension drain away. I had a peaceful dinner and turned in early. Next day, I was leaving for Lukla to catch my flight to Kathmandu from where I would take an onward flight to the Kangchenjunga region.

En Route to Kangchenjunga

"This is Cami!" Anu presented my porter to me as I ate breakfast next morning. He was in his late teens with straight black hair and a friendly smile and he could speak some English. Soon, I called goodbye to Anu through the kitchen door and Cami and I set off for Lukla. He shouldered my big backpack with ease and I lifted my smaller day sack. It was the same one in which I'd carried Cyril's ashes to Robin Hood's Cave on Stanage Edge. Every day, when I put it on my back, I felt a physical warmth from it.

The trail to Lukla made a steep descent to the Dudh Kosi river before a further, gradual descent down the valley. I struggled to match Cami's fast pace and several times he had to pause while I caught up. At the bottom of the initial descent the trail crossed the river by means of a narrow suspension bridge. My heart almost stopped when I saw it.

It was a good bridge by Himalayan standards. It was five planks wide and there was a wire with struts forming each side. I stood at the end and realised that, however much I dreaded it, I had to either cross it or walk back 12 days the way I'd come. I asked Cami to stand at the end and keep anyone else from coming on the bridge while I was on it, making it bounce up and down. So I started across, concentrating on the middle plank and looking neither right nor left. I coached myself: "Come on, Dyson, you can do this. You're doing fine, just keep going!" Suddenly, the middle plank was missing and I felt my muscles freeze as I saw the river rushing whitely over the jagged rocks below. For a long moment I was fixed to the spot; and then I heard a voice say, "Get on with it!" It was the gruff, no-nonsense voice Cyril used when there was no alternative to a particular course of action and it prompted me to step quickly over the gap and walk on, once again focusing on the middle plank. I made it to the end of the bridge, overcome with sweat and relief. Cami crossed it as though he did it every day of his life, which he probably did. We followed the trail down to the water level and I looked back up at the bridge – a narrow ribbon strung out 200 feet over the boulders and white water below. I felt rather pleased with myself.

We stopped for soup and tea at Phakding, one of the nine settlements along this stretch of trail. On our way again, we talked about the plants that we saw and I showed Cami a shamrock with yellow flowers. We listened to cuckoos and crows and grasshoppers with enormous clicking sounds. Cami enquired delicately if I had any children, to which I replied in the negative and then told him about Cyril. He looked at me with an understanding beyond his years, reminding me of Greg.

At Lukla, Cami took me to the lodging house near the airstrip. It was run by a Sherpani called Shasti who also acted as agent for the trekking company in Kathmandu who were responsible for my travel arrangements. There was no sign of her on my arrival, but her sister Menala, who was working in the kitchen, assured me that my flight to Kathmandu had been confirmed for the next day. I paid Cami off and he seemed pleased as we shook hands and said goodbye.

My room at Shasti's house was cold and dark; I spent a depressing night there and was glad when morning came and it was time to go to the airstrip. Shasti herself escorted me, dressed up in full Sherpani costume, while a woman underling carried my rucksack. By the time Shasti checked me in and gave me my air ticket, she had impressed me as one of the laziest, greediest people I'd ever met. She did no actual work and kept asking me for money.

At 8 am the flight was cancelled because the grass runway was too muddy. There was a communal frustration among the dozen waiting passengers and I was worried because of my ongoing flight to the Kangchenjunga region the next day. The official told me to reconfirm at the Royal Nepal office that afternoon. I stood there at a loss and then spotted Cami in the crowd. I waved to him and he came to join me. He offered to take me to his sister's lodging house, Panorama Lodge, and I accepted.

Cami's sister gave me a small clean room and I sat on the edge of my bed thinking about the morning's events. A gentle tap on the door post made me look up. It was Pawa Temba, Cami's brother-in-law. He said, "If you want to go to Kathmandu today, I can get you on the helicopter for 90 dollars!" I hesitated for a few seconds before I said, "Okay, but I'll need a refund on my air ticket, I can't afford both." Pawa said, "We can fix it!"

He fixed everything. He retrieved my flight coupon from the check-in man in the radio tower and most of my excess baggage money. Then, leaning on the dry stone wall at the end of the runway, I signed 90 dollars' worth of traveller's cheques for Pawa, a man I hardly knew. But, like Anu and Cami, he inspired confidence with his open, gentle manner – and he was rather handsome.

No ticket or receipt were issued and no helicopter appeared. For a while, I felt uneasy, but then we heard the chap-chap of the rotor blades as the Russian helicopter hovered up the runway and touched down lightly on the unloading ground. Once the San Miguel cargo had been unloaded, Cami and I put my luggage aboard. I gave him a generous tip as we shook hands. Good-hearted and resourceful, he had helped me solve my problem.

Flying in a helicopter with a reputation for falling out of the sky was exciting but it was even more exciting to be flying in the foothills of the Himalayas. The route to Kathmandu took us through narrow valleys on the sides of which I could see cultivated fields close to hill settlements. We emerged on to the Kathmandu plain and landed close to the domestic terminal at the international airport. I managed to cadge a lift into the city with an elderly American couple and they obligingly dropped me off at Hotel Sherpa.

I had a shock when I looked in the mirror in my room. My skin was a walnut brown and although my split lips were healing, my burnt nose had skin flaking off it. My hair looked wild – the natural wave refused to lie flat and I'd long since given up on it. I spent 20 minutes scrubbing myself clean in the hot shower.

That evening I finalised my travel arrangements in the bar with Bickram Pandy, one of the owners of the trekking agency. I would have an early morning flight to Biratnagar, an overnight stay there, and a further flight to Suketar, the airstrip for Taplejung, a large town near Kangchenjunga. Later, having survived four weeks in rough conditions, I indulged myself in the luxurious restaurant of Hotel

Sherpa. I ordered the national dish, daal bhaat. It consisted of lentil soup, white rice and curried vegetables. I ate from a marble table lit by a gold lamp. But it was here, ironically, that I caught an infection caused by poor hygiene. It was giardiasis and it attacked my bowel with gusto.

On the flight to Biratnagar, which is close to the southern border of Nepal with India, I was the only woman and, apart from an American called Chuck, the only white person. Biratnagar itself was dirty, noisy, crowded and very hot. The infection took hold and I spent a large part of the afternoon racing to the toilet in my hotel room. Gokail Bistra, the sophisticated owner of the hotel, could not understand my persistent refusal to eat. Late in the afternoon he brought a young man into the hotel garden where I sat under the shade of a tree. Temba was to be my translator and guide for the rest of my trip. He and I sat there making a harsh appraisal of each other. He was of medium height with thick, black hair and spots on his face. He showed no interest in the task ahead of him. For his part, he saw a sickly, older woman who had no smile or enthusiasm and he was stuck with me for the next ten days. Grudgingly, we agreed a time to meet the following morning. I had to suppress a strong urge to cancel the trip.

The flight to Suketar surprised Temba and me. He was excited at being on his first flight and when we stepped on to the grass runway at Suketar, I was relieved by the cool breeze of high places – we were back up to 8,500 feet. The clean, cool air reduced the feeling of nausea.

Taplejung, my base for the next ten days, was 2,000 feet down the mountain from Suketar. As Temba and I carried our rucksacks down the hard mud trail, we became the focus of intense curiosity for the people we passed. I watched bemused as one man's jaw dropped open. His head swivelled round after me, the jaw still groundwards. I wondered what Temba was thinking, but he began to win my respect because he showed no embarrassment and stayed loyally with me all the way.

We reached the edge of the town and went down the main street looking for Namgey Hotel, named after Temba's uncle. We found it on a small side street. It was built of stone, two storeys high with a thatched roof. Once we were inside the darkened dining room, someone pulled back a window shutter and sunlight flooded in to show a Sherpa man and woman looking at us curiously: Temba's uncle, Namgey and his aunt, Bhutia. In a moment, she had disappeared into the kitchen at the back and was making Sherpa tea. Namgey spoke to me in English and I arranged rooms for Temba and myself. We shook hands on the deal. I watched him as I drank my tea. He was tall for a Sherpa and his hair was more like that of an Afro-Caribbean. His Tibetan eyes gave him away. They were a dark brown with such a depth of understanding that the words "eyes that know everything" went through my mind. Temba left us to confirm our return flight to Kathmandu in ten days' time.

I said to Namgey, "I want to see Kangchenjunga." He motioned me out on to the front porch and pointed far up the lush valley. "Go to Patibahra! There you will see Kangchenjunga." It looked a long way and when Temba came back he translated Namgey's estimation of the distance – 12 miles along a hilly trail through the jungle with an altitude gain of nearly 7,000 feet.

That evening I sat on the balcony outside my room and wrote my journal. After the events of the last two days, I was glad to be settled in one place. I thought of the voices I'd heard at awkward moments, sometimes seeming to be my own and sometimes Cyril's. It was his direct Yorkshire voice that came out of my mouth when anyone around me wasn't being straight with me. I realised that the intense loneliness that I'd experienced in Namche had receded, mainly because now I at least had a base and people to be with.

Patibahra

Next afternoon I made the decision to go to Patibahra and see Kangchenjunga. I sat in the dining room with Temba, Namgey and Namgey's son, Kasang, and discussed the Buddhist pilgrimage route to the 13,000 feet summit of Patibahra. Temba was keen and soon we were on the main street of Taplejung looking for a shop that sold dried food and bottled water. The expedition would take three days and there was no water above Kedi, the last settlement at 10,000 feet. When we returned to Namgey's, Kasang asked if he could join us on the journey. I agreed – two minders would be better than one.

The dining room took on the air of a packing post. Bhutia's smiling face kept appearing at the kitchen hatch as she passed in small plates to Kasang and Temba who carefully packed the offerings of rice and maize into plastic bags. Bhutia then prepared food for Kasang to carry in his rucksack. Namgey kept chipping in with his comments. Temba said, "We have to go back up to Suketar and on then into the jungle to Kedi. There is a shepherd's shack there where we can shelter. I hope we have enough water!"

We started the next morning on the rocky trail up to Suketar where we paused for refreshments in a seedy lodging house next to the airstrip. From there we walked in an easterly direction along the top of a broad, grassy ridge until we reached what the locals called the 'jungle'. It had a dense growth of rhododendron trees in full leaf with heavy moisture dripping off every branch and trunk. The undergrowth was thinner. The trail followed a tortuous route that wound over numerous ridges and, after eight hard hours, we reached the summer settlement at Kedi.

There was an empty shack close to the trail and Kasang said, "I'll go and find the owner and ask if we can use it." He disappeared into the trees and minutes later he was back with an invitation: "The shepherd said would we like to spend the night at his shack and cook on his fire?" Temba and I followed him along a small trail into the jungle until we came to a clearing at the back of which, nestling into the hillside, was the shepherd's shack.

It was 60 feet wide and made of bamboo cane matting tied together to form three walls – a back and two sides and the front was open to the elements. The roof was a light thatch. Inside, it was divided into three parts, the middle one being for the humans. There was a cemented hearth with a log fire burning brightly and a brass pot bubbling on top with a mixture of rice, milk and curd. Around the hearth, on three sides, was the living accommodation where people sat on cane matting. At the back of the fire there was a storage area for mattresses, blankets and spare clothes. The two outer sections of the house were for the animals. In the left section seven sheep sheltered inside a lightly fenced area, while the right section housed six young goats and a calf which kept bawling for its mother. She, apparently, was grazing elsewhere.

The shepherd, Calindro, came forward to meet us. He was my height, thin and raggedly dressed but his huge, brown eyes had a meltingly soft expression, as did his two younger brothers who stood watching shyly from behind the fire. All three looked at me with intense curiosity.

The only thing I insisted on that evening was a place to sleep by myself. Calindro pointed to one side of the fire. Temba and Kasang were accommodated at the back of the hearth, the two brothers slept in the storage area, and Calindro had the third side. I sat on my sleeping bag as Temba cooked our noodles on the fire and the two brothers sat near me, watching my every move. The noodles satisfied our deep physical hunger, caused by hours in the open air.

It was a strange sensation to be lying in an open shack at 10,000 feet in the Himalayas listening to the shrill singing and fast rhythm of Indian pop music from Calindro's unexpected transistor. Once the radio was switched off, the silence was as deep as the dark. All I could see were the trees on the edge of the clearing silhouetted against a black, star-filled sky. Eventually, I fell asleep, listening to the slow, deep breathing of the cow whose resting place was separated from mine by a section of cane matting.

I woke at 3 am for an early start on the long 3,000 feet ascent to the summit of Patibahra and, from the moment we said goodbye to Calindro and the others, I struggled with my breathing in the increasing altitude. The endless forest alongside the trail blocked our view but at last we came to a sign that read, 'Take it slowly – you're almost there!'

We reached the tree-covered summit together and stood at the door of the temple building. From my rucksack I took out a picture of Cyril and myself, taken on Mount Parnassus in Greece. Temba said, "How long ago? You look young!" I replied, "Four years," and burst into tears. This bursting into tears on the tops of Himalayan mountains was becoming a habit, and made me aware of how much grief I still had for Cyril. His death had, indirectly, brought me to Nepal and grief was the undoubted cause of these emotional outbursts. Now, my two minders looked at me and didn't know what to say. When I calmed down, we moved on into the temple.

We entered it through a stone arch to find that the building was open to the sky. Dozens of bells, donated by pilgrims, hung all the way round the six foot walls. On one side of the temple was an altar made of stone and covered with flowers and petals offered in sacrifice by Hindus and Buddhists. On the other side was a small alcove with a scarlet area on the floor in front of it. Hundreds of flies and wasps buzzed round it. Temba said, "That red is the blood from young goats that Hindus kill here. They let the blood run for a short time before cooking and eating the goat."

He and Kasang proceeded with their Buddhist ceremony. They produced the little bags of rice and maize which Bhutia had given them and they scattered their offerings on the altar and then, with great reverence, lit short incense sticks which filled the air with a delicate odour. They made a gesture towards the altar and then stood in silence. At that point I went out of the temple and yelled "CYRIL!" at the top of my voice. That was my prayer. The others made no comment about my shouting but Temba approached me and gently made a red mark on my forehead as a sign that I had made the pilgrimage. He passed me one of the red Buddhist prayer ribbons from the altar to take away with me. Finally, he placed a purple flower behind my ear. His actions were so gentle and inclusive that I was deeply moved.

Once we had finished, we sat outside and ate the flat bread that Namgey had provided and drank from our limited supply of bottled water. We felt close to each other: after our long journey, we had reached our summit together. I had almost forgotten that the other main reason for the journey was so that I could see Kangchenjunga. We didn't see anything of it as the low cloud and mist swirled around the summit of Patibahra the whole time we were there. Now, it seemed unimportant.

The return journey brought a pleasant surprise – as the altitude decreased, so did my weariness and we made it back the same day to Suketar where we spent the night in the seedy lodging house.

Final Days In the Himalayas

However seedy the lodging house was at Suketar, I was glad to reach it after 10 hours' walking. The dark dining room was filled with listless men who loitered at the tables or leaned on the doorframe. Kasang spoke to a bent old woman in the kitchen at the back and surprised me by saying, "This house belongs to my cousins. That woman is my grandmother, Namgey's mother." I looked at her tired worn face but I couldn't connect the mean, greedy eyes to the open dignity of Namgey.

The next morning Bhutia welcomed us back to Namgey Hotel and the dining room echoed to the sounds of Kasang's and Temba's lively account of our journey. Afterwards, I went to sit in the back yard next to Bhutia and sensed I was accepted when she let me help her shell peas for the evening meal. Suddenly she said, "Hukhuraako!" and pointed to a chicken scratching the ground. "Chicken!" I replied and we both laughed. Then she looked at my clothes – I was wearing a T-shirt and tracksuit bottoms. I reached under my collar and pulled out a bra strap. She smiled and reached under her silk blouse for the strap of her cotton vest. We laughed again. I showed her the elastic waistband of my knickers and she showed me the top of her long underskirt. We giggled like teenagers. For several hours we sat drinking tea, sharing sweets and having a crazy, stilted conversation. Later I saw Namgey and Bhutia's mutual pleasure at the sight of each other when he returned home from market at 5 pm.

That evening in the dining room I spoke to Temba about my wish to research the lives of the people of Nepal, especially the women. Soon

Namgey and Bhutia agreed to help me. Next afternoon, while I sat writing my journal on the balcony, Namgey came and sat at my feet. We talked about the trekking business and his hotel. He had land up at Suketar and wanted to build a second hotel, but there was no help from the government – he would have to do it himself. Although Namgey gave me further insights into his business, I really wanted to know the family history. My chance came next morning when Temba joined Namgey, Bhutia and me in the cool dining room. The story had romance, tragedy and family steadfastness as Temba translated for us.

Namgey was the son of a lama who had fallen in love with a young woman whom he married against his father's wishes. Namgey was born a year later but the grandfather exerted such pressure that the young couple divorced. Namgey stayed with his mother, the woman up at Suketar. Both his parents later re-married and had new families. When I compared him to his mother, I concluded that he inherited his dignity and intelligence from his lama father.

Bhutia had grown up in the same village as Namgey and liked him because he was kind to his mother. She had been free to choose her husband and the marriage was a happy one. They had six children, four daughters and two sons, of whom Kasang was the eldest. Although Namgey and Bhutia had no formal education themselves, they had made an early decision to give their children the best education they could afford and all four daughters had completed college courses in Kathmandu. As parents, they were satisfied with their efforts – all four daughters were married with families. Kasang, who had just completed his secondary education, would be going to

college in Kathmandu in a few months' time and the younger brother
was still at school. I had the feeling that Namgey and Bhutia had
achieved what most people wish for – a good family and a decent
living. They seemed to regard education as the key and my university
education and teaching career gave me status in their eyes, as well as
in the eyes of the people of Taplejung, among whom I seemed to be
acquiring a doubtful fame.

Next day, I went with Temba and Kasang to visit two local schools,
a primary and a secondary. At the primary school, a woman teacher
enquired if I was a university professor. I was honest and said no, but
four other teachers, two men and two women, who came along the
corridor where we were standing, all looked at me with awe in their
eyes – or perhaps it was amazement at my strange, western appearance.
At the secondary school, I disappointed a woman teacher because I
could not promise to supply the money to repair the school plumbing
system. Overall, these teachers told me a lot about the schools.
Education had become compulsory for all just a few years before and
education and employment opportunities for women teachers had
opened up in the district, mainly due to the appointment of 200 women
teachers to the primary schools. Usually, girls were married off at 15
and that was the end of their education.

The following day Temba took me to visit a private boarding school
where the pupils were all boys. He told me that any money available to
pay for private education was spent on the sons of families – they were
seen as a better investment than daughters who went to live with their
in-laws once they were married. In time, no doubt, private education

will become more available to girls and in this Namgey and Bhutia seemed years ahead of their time.

As I approached the end of my stay in Taplejung, I had a strong sense of relief that I was going home to Sheffield. Anxiety and homesickness were taking their toll – nightly, I was having panic attacks and daily I longed to see the hills of the Peak District. I was getting desperate for something familiar. Since I had arrived in Taplejung, I had neither seen nor spoken to a single white person. Namgey and Bhutia were as kind as anyone could be, but I was alone and a long way from home. Only I was responsible for myself and at night when I went to bed I thought about what would happen if I fell ill. My stomach would tighten with anxiety and then my legs and feet would twitch and shake with a tension I couldn't at first identify. I came to realise it was happening when I felt anxious about being so far from home. I also realised I was at the limits of my coping ability.

Late on the last afternoon I cheerfully packed my rucksack and went down to the dining room. Bhutia appeared from the kitchen where she was making a special dinner in my honour. I smiled at her and asked for a tongba, a Tibetan beer. She returned minutes later with the round wooden barrel and hollow cane poking through the lid through which the beer was sucked – the beer was made by pouring boiling water over pulverised millet beans. I perched myself cross-legged on the cushioned bench against the wall and took a long suck on the cane. Gradually, the mild tongba beer added to my growing sense of well-being. I noticed a man sitting on a chair near the window enjoying a glass of rakshi. He caught my eye and raised his glass in salutation.

"Are you here on holiday?" he asked.

As we talked I looked at him curiously. He was taller than me with weathered light brown skin and probably in his mid-50s. His manner was courteous and friendly as he told me his name was Lamsal and he came from Kathmandu. I was charmed by the unexpected male attention. It may have been the relaxing effect of the tongba that led me to tell him about Cyril and how angry I still felt that he been taken from me. I also told him I wanted to be a writer.

Lamsal's response was of such understanding and kindness that the tears started to flow – the tears that come when you're under stress and someone is kind. When he saw my distress, he pressed me no further but told me about himself. He said, "My wife died of cancer four years ago and I felt very bad but, eventually, I volunteered for employment on a project and it helped me find purpose and satisfaction."

Unasked, he gave me his thoughts. He said, "Let go of Cyril and move on, it's unavoidable that he won't return. You will remember him but you must let go and move on. Stay adventurous and keep writing, but also find yourself a job in the community that you can commit yourself to. One tragedy doesn't finish a life – you have to go on and find other good things. You must live again." He concluded his uplifting speech with an invitation to join him for dinner. Regretfully, I had to decline because I was dining with Namgey and Bhutia but I let him buy me a glass of rakshi. With deep and genuine goodwill, we raised our glasses.

I joined Namgey, Bhutia, Temba and Kasang at a big round table for our special dinner. Bhutia produced lentil sauce, vegetable curry, chicken curry and boiled rice. It was a feast in my honour, but I couldn't do it justice. The problem was the chicken. Earlier in the afternoon while Bhutia and I were sitting in the back yard, she had suddenly grabbed a chicken that came too close, wrung its neck and placed it on the table next to us with its head lolling to one side. She gave me a big smile and said, "Dinner!"

She had cooked the chicken in its entirety, apart from the feathers and claws. I pulled a few pieces out of the dish and felt my stomach heave as the yellow-green string of entrails clung to the spoon. I placed the pieces on the edge of my plate. I saw the offence in Bhutia's eyes but there was nothing I could do. I thought of the intrepid travellers I'd read about who seemed able to consume almost anything so as not to offend their host and I felt ashamed that I wasn't one of them – Bhutia was honouring me with her cooking, and I seemed to be throwing it back in her face. If I had eaten it, that is exactly what I would have done. However, her good nature won through and the warm feeling that had grown between us during the last ten days returned. As the evening ended, I looked around the table with genuine affection for the four people who had helped to steer me through my time in Taplejung. I would miss them, especially Bhutia.

At 5 am the following morning a sad little group gathered on the porch of Namgey Hotel. Bhutia presented Temba and myself with two prayer scarves as gifts and blessings to take with us. Feeling honoured, I kissed her on the cheek. She accepted the gesture and looked sadly back at me. I shook hands with Namgey who gave me a slow, friendly smile and wished me a safe journey home. It was time to go. I looked back at the two of them as I turned into the main street – Bhutia was wiping a tear from her cheek.

The flight to Biratnagar took off as planned and once we arrived I made a swift farewell to Temba who, from such an unpromising beginning, had performed well as a guide and translator. He had to rush off to catch his bus home to his hill village and my onward flight to Kathmandu took off an hour later.

My last night there was spent in the comfortable Hotel Tiloch. I went out to buy a few presents for people at home and I walked the streets with much more confidence than when I had first arrived. I no longer expected that someone would mug me and I found asking for discount on the prices now to be a matter of course – the Nepalis think you a fool if you don't.

On the flight home next day I sat alone – the only spare seat was next to me. I spent much of the flight thinking about my adventures, with their moments of danger and how I'd come through unscathed, of the kindness of strangers and the closeness of Cyril. I thought of Lamsal and his words of encouragement: "Stay adventurous and keep writing. Find a job to commit yourself to in the community." I thought about God, or whatever God is. I felt as though I'd been given a double dose of kindness to show that there was good in the world even after the pain and anger of losing Cyril. I said my first prayer in three years that wasn't full of anger and hatred. And I began to wonder what I might do next.

PART TWO

A Woman in Flight

The Sheffield Himalayas

Lamsal's words haunted me throughout the summer. I had not envisaged such an emotional reaction to the end of my Himalayan adventures. I was thrilled to see my mother, relieved to see off the end of the giardiasis in my own home, and delighted to rejoin my friends at the running club. Even the panic attacks disappeared within days of my return. So why did I feel so flat and restless?

Most of it was caused by anticlimax. There was nothing to challenge or absorb me. The Himalayas had raised me up and now I felt empty. I might have expected the feeling to dissipate over the passing weeks and to arrive back at my normal frame of mind in Sheffield, but it didn't happen. Instead, I sank lower into a boredom-induced depression. I found no satisfaction in the aimless, comfortable life I had come back to and it seemed an insane contrast to the life of the Sherpas who lived with the minimum of possessions. I thought about a piece of string I'd left on the ground outside my tent at Chamlang Base Camp the day after Mera Peak. Next morning I saw the same piece of string holding a huge porter load together. I started to feel that my home, modest by English standards, was full of clutter; but however much I disposed of, I didn't feel any better. I had to find a purpose. Lamsal's words came back to me again: "Stay adventurous and keep writing. Find yourself a job in the community that you can commit yourself to." By the end of August the only thing that made any sense was the recurring thought of following my second dream of becoming a pilot, despite my mother's anxieties. Early in September I decided to go for it. I didn't know then that becoming a pilot would result in things happening that I hadn't bargained for.

Within a few days I found my way to Netherthorpe Airfield, three miles west of Worksop in Nottinghamshire and 12 miles from where I lived. The narrow lane leading to Netherthorpe wound its way through trees before passing several farm buildings and emerging into a flat open area. On the three foot fence on the left was a small triangular sign with a climbing jet on it and I laughed as I passed it. For the first time since I came home from Nepal, I felt alive. A few yards further on I caught sight of the airfield. Over the low hedge on the right was a grass runway stretching away towards a large wood at the far end. Then a row of hangars came into view. A tall pole with a billowing windsock stood on the right of the entrance to the potholed car park and immediately ahead were two buildings with a paved area between them. I parked close to the one on the right, a single-storey wooden building with a 'Reception' notice nailed to the eaves. Taking a sharp breath, I pushed open the wooden door to see two men sitting opposite on an old leather sofa which was in keeping with the rough industrial squares carpeting the floor of the reception area. A third man stood leaning against the edge of a deep waist-high shelf and a yellow labrador lay belly down with its head resting on its front paws. The three men and the dog looked up at me as I entered and the man who was standing said, "Can we help you?" I burst out, "I've come to find out about learning to fly!" It was a statement of serious intent – no longer a dream. The man straightened up and said, "Let me show you around and tell you all about it!"

He introduced himself as Ian Drake and as we walked along the paved area behind the adjoining building which was the clubhouse, he talked flying and aircraft. I heard little of what he said – the excitement was mounting inside me. He pointed to the two-seater Cessna aircraft parked beyond the low wall of the public enclosure. "We use those for training," he said.

We followed a shaft of sunlight through the part-open doors of the first hangar and, in the shadows, I could make out eight small aircraft parked close together, wings and propellers inches apart. The hangar was still and silent. Ian beckoned me across to a low-winged yellow aircraft and pointed into the cabin. For the first time in my life, I saw a cockpit.

I seemed to feel my brain scramble inside my skull. For several seconds, I was beyond speech. I heard nothing that Ian said, just stood gaping at the instrument panel, the joystick and the two side-by-side seats. I had waited 36 years for this moment, and I wasn't disappointed.

Ian's voice filtered through the haze as he rattled on about light aircraft and flying safety and, with great reluctance, I followed him back to reception. Firm ambition had taken hold as I approached the glass-topped counter and booked myself a trial lesson for two weeks later. Every prospective pilot has a trial lesson to ensure they are going to be all right in a light aircraft. I was going for a short holiday to Ireland and knew I would savour the delicious anticipation of my first flying lesson when I came back.

The day of my lesson – Wednesday 30 September 1994 – was a fine autumn day with high streaks of cloud across a blue sky. I arrived far too early and was sent to wait in the clubhouse next door. As I waited, looking at my watch every two minutes, my stomach was winding itself into a large knot. When the time eventually came, I filled in the inevitable form and, minutes later, was walking out with Ian Drake to a maroon and white Cessna 152.

I sat in the left-hand seat, the captain's seat in true aviation tradition, and as Ian checked that my headset and harness were secure, the knot of tension in my stomach gave way to a feeling of adrenalin. He climbed in the right-hand side, settled himself and fired up the engine. It shocked me at first that I was so close to the throbbing engine; even through my headset I could hear it. I felt it humming through the airframe and watched the faint circle of the spinning propeller through the windscreen. Ian taxied to the hold for runway 24, the main runway at Netherthorpe, completed his checks and turned on to the runway. He pushed the throttle fully open and we were away.

I looked sideways out of the window as the grass dropped away and we passed over the lane at the end of the runway. Ian climbed the aircraft past the wood on the left. He carried on climbing as we headed north-west towards a village where I had spent four miserable years as a brand new teacher at a local comprehensive school. Ian circled the Cessna over it and I pretended to drop flour bombs on it while hissing through the microphone. Laughing, he turned the aircraft towards Sheffield and soon we were circling over my house at Intake. It took a concentrated effort to identify my little spot in the world amongst the jumble of roads and trees. When I found it, I called into the microphone "Hello, house!" Ian turned the Cessna on to a easterly heading, climbing all the while. At 4,000 feet he said suddenly, "It's all yours!" I took the control column in my hands with the same feeling of near terror as when I first drove a car, but I couldn't bottle out and made a quick decision to do a full 360 degree turn. I was so tense that I held the control yoke on the top of the column like a vice as the aircraft nosed around the horizon. After an age, I said to Ian in a tight voice, "Am I there yet?" He grinned at me, said "Yes!" and retook control. He set a return course for Netherthorpe.

The next few minutes were close to perfection. For a while we flew through the pure clean air towards the distant eastern horizon, bathed in blue. The shades of blue were beautiful – there were elongated areas of translucent turquoise, sky blue and blue-grey. The air had a glow like the glow you see in high mountains and snowfields where so much sunlight is reflected back into space. I could see the white billows of smoke rising from the power stations on the River Trent and below me were thousands of acres of agricultural land, the surface of which was patterned with hedgerows, lanes and clumps of woodland. I had only one thought, "This is where I want to be!" Then another thought occurred, "This is like the Himalayas, yet we're over Sheffield and I can get here often!" Later I called it the moment of commitment: whatever happened, I was going to be a pilot and fly in the Sheffield Himalayas.

The final gem of the lesson came as we approached the airfield. Ian pulled the throttle closed to show me that the aircraft could land without power. The descent was steep and quiet as we glided in on final approach to land and I watched the runway and the white concrete 24 numbers come closer through the windscreen. Suddenly they were rushing up at us and and I realised we were going in nose first. I shut my eyes and waited for the crash. It didn't come. After a few seconds, I opened one eye and looked at Ian who was pulling back on the control column to lift the nose of the aircraft and to present its wheels to the ground for a smooth touch down. When I saw we were down safely, my stomach unknotted itself and I laughed a long, delighted laugh. "Brilliant!" I said to Ian.

Five minutes later I was back in reception facing the man behind the desk, booking four lessons, one a week for the next four weeks.

"November, November, Downwind!"

Six days later I started flying training in earnest. I'd just bought my pilot log book, flying manual and aeroplane check list in the flight centre when Ian came into reception with a mug of coffee. I had nominated to learn to fly with him as he made flying fun. I watched him while he drank. In his late 50s, he had a military bearing with a full head of brown hair and dark brown eyes. He must have sensed my impatience, because soon we were on our way out to the maroon and white Cessna 152 in which I'd had my trial lesson. Its registration was G-BRNN or Golf-Bravo Romeo November November.

The first thing I learned to do was the 'walk-around', the visual pre-flight inspection that a pilot makes before flying; but I really wanted to get airborne. When Ian said, "We'll leave the rest of this for a wet day. Let's go flying!" I asked, "Can we go out over the Peak District?" He did the take-off and climb out and before long we were over the Derwent Valley and close to the edge of Manchester airspace. As we flew, Ian started to teach me the effects of the aeroplane controls. Initially, I found it hard: I am not a technical person and I had no flying background whatsoever, only the burning desire to be a pilot, which carried me through my flying training.

The problem with learning to fly was that I had to think about several things at once, which was difficult when I had only a hazy idea of what each thing meant. It helped that most of the early lessons were out over the Peak District – it was a familiar environment in which to learn. Ian taught me to fly straight and level, to turn, to make the aeroplane climb and descend, to fly at different speeds and altitudes. He taught me the use of the throttle, the trim, and the flaps. He taught me how to make the aeroplane stall and recover. The next task was the take-off. I remember the day I made my first serious attempt at it.

I did the last of my checks at the hold for runway 24, taxied on to it and turned to face the far end. Ian said, "Stick back, give it full throttle, keep it moving and keep it straight." November November's engine gave full belt and we rumbled over the bumpy grass surface, gaining airspeed. I recognised the moment of flying speed when the bumping stopped and I glanced sideways out of my window to see the wheels still spinning and the grass falling away. As the aeroplane rose, so did my spirits. I was one step nearer to being in charge for myself. We climbed out to the Pennines in the west and soon ran into an area of turbulence. Suddenly, the needle on the vertical speed indicator went right off the dial. Ian said, "We've hit a rising thermal and we're climbing faster than this aeroplane can do under engine power!" We burst out on top of the thin cloud at 5,000 feet and it was the most beautiful sight I'd seen so far. Everywhere was a sea of white cloud, and above it was an arc of crisp blue sky with a bright watery sun that nearly blinded us.

Below, through large gaps in the cloud, I could see Rivelin Valley and the A57 Snake road curving westwards through the Pennines. I saw the solitary rock at Moscar and Stanage Edge stretching southwards. I looked along it in the distance and thought about Robin Hood's Cave from where I had scattered Cyril's ashes. I wondered what he would have thought of my new life. At that moment, Ian shouted at me for messing up the powered descent procedure that I was supposed to be practising. I became nervous and did what I often do when I'm in a tight spot – I started giggling. This made him shout even more, "You handle this aeroplane like a shovel!" Now I laughed out loud and, once started, I couldn't stop. Ian roared, "You're supposed to be feminine and gentle!" By now I was helpless and almost let go of the control column. He glared at me and I was rendered speechless. In the end, he had to give in to laughter. When we had recovered some composure, we practised stall recovery before heading back to Netherthorpe. When we landed, I said, "Thanks for that. It was the best yet." Ian smiled and said, "But you always say that!"

It was true. Each lesson seemed more enjoyable than the last and I talked about it incessantly to anyone who would listen. I poured it out to my running buddies at Totley AC and they listened to me with remarkable tolerance. It was just as well, because there was no one else to tell. That was the real downside of learning to fly.

Every Wednesday afternoon I sped down the country lanes to my lessons. As I drove, I often laughed aloud in delight at the treat to come. When I turned into the car park I'd look for November November – I almost regarded it as my aeroplane – and once I was in the flight centre, I'd become impatient to be airborne. Going home was a different matter. As I climbed out of November November at the end of the lesson, I came back to the reality of being earthborne. I felt drab as I drove away and half a mile down the lane I was often in tears, mainly because there was no one at home with whom to share the great feeling of flight. There was an empty house where I would spend the long dark evening alone. It was like that for weeks.

I told my mother what I had been up to three weeks after I started lessons. She growled at me, "I don't want to have to come and scrape up the pieces. Well, it's your money and your life." I could only agree with her. I hadn't said much to Cyril either. Every day I looked at his picture on the coffee table in my lounge. If I was troubled, I'd stand in front of it and tell him about it. These one-sided conversations were short and ended with a request – "Look after me!" Yet, when I looked at his picture and thought about the flying, I always felt guilty. It was something he wouldn't have done: once, when I'd suggested the possibility to him, long before he became ill, he rejected the idea, saying we couldn't afford it. I felt he considered it to be a complete waste of time and money. Then I would think to myself – "Well, you're gone and I'm here. It's up to me!" I became aware of detaching from the grief and longing for Cyril. Unconsciously, I was making a new life – my life for myself. As if to confirm this, Ian told me next lesson that I was ready to start training in the circuit. This is where the basic flying skills that every student pilot needs are learned – take-off, climb out, climbing turn, level flight, descending, descending turn and landing. He added, "It will be all the skills you have learned so far and you'll have to do them all in five minutes!"

It was now December and I gave myself a 'Cyril' present for Christmas – what I would have asked Cyril for if he'd been alive. This year it was three flying lessons in a week. On the first one a strong wind made circuits impossible. I still wanted to go flying and told Ian I'd like to practise descending and levelling. I'm glad I have a passion for inessentials. The flight was the most beautiful of my flying training.

We flew westwards towards the Pennines. Thick lumps of cloud hung over the Peak District, casting dark shadows over the heather-covered hills. There were rectangles of snow in places where the heather had been burned in the autumn. I was surprised at the experience of flying through snow flurries where the world went a pale grey and little white flakes shot past the window. We talked as we flew over Derwent Edge, along which I'd walked a few days earlier. Away to the south-west I could see snow-covered Lose Hill and the trail winding up Mam Tor. I raised the nose of November November to climb over clouds ahead of us, but Ian cautioned me about getting too high. Instead, we moved towards the sun through a gap in a heavy snow cloud. The sun was hiding behind another tower of cloud. Above us was the cold, yellow-blue of a clear winter's evening. Ian said, "Anyone who fails to be moved by this must be dead." I told him I'd been learning the poem 'High Flight' by John Gillespie Magee, one of my all-time favourite poems. Spontaneously, Ian started to recite it and I joined in. The last three lines sent a shiver down my spine:

> 'And while with silent lifting mind I've trod
> The high, untrespassed sanctity of space,
> Reached out my hand and touched the face of God.'

In silence, we sat side by side and flew towards the setting sun.

After Christmas, circuit training began in earnest. The circuit means the rectangular pattern that surrounds every airfield and allows for an orderly flow of traffic. Circuit training means acquiring all the skills needed to fly the circuit. It would all soon be made clear, Ian promised me. On the first lesson in the New Year, we took off from runway 24 and he talked me through it.

We climbed out straight ahead from the runway, alongside the edge of Whitwell Woods, until we reached 500 feet. At that point we made a climbing turn left on to the crosswind leg over the woods and levelled out at 800 feet. Ian told me to point the nose to the base of Whitwell chimney and use that as my landmark. When we reached the edge of the woods, we made another left hand turn on to the downwind leg, passing over Steetley works. Ian called, "November, November, downwind, 24 left" and I did my pre-landing checks. The most important of these were to make sure the brakes were off and our seat belts were fastened tightly. At the end of the downwind leg, just beyond Steetley works, we turned left on to base leg and then set up the aeroplane for landing. This meant slowing it down and letting down some flap, and descending at 500 feet a minute. Once we were abeam the big white concrete numbers on the runway, we turned left on to final approach to land. We were descending at 55 knots – 60 miles per hour – and 500 feet a minute. The runway numbers were rushing up at us and I panicked. How did we avoid crashing? Ian took control for the touch down and 'flared', which meant raising the nose as the aeroplane was just a few feet off the ground. This ensured that contact with the ground was controlled and smooth. My tension evaporated and I couldn't stop smiling. That was what flying was about for me – pure joy and a total challenge. But for a long time the landing eluded me. It was the 'flare' which confused me – judging the moment of when to raise the nose. If I flared too high it would be a heavy landing, and if I flared too low it meant excess weight on the nose wheel.

For the next three months we did 'circuits and bumps'. I flew the circuit and tried to do the landing, with a variety of interesting results, none of which were out of the text book. Ian earned his instructor's pay and so did Martyn Webster, another instructor with whom I sometimes flew when Ian was not available. Tall and dark, he was the antithesis of Ian. Where Ian was lively and chatty, Martyn was quiet and thoughtful. He didn't shout, but allowed me to work things out for myself and, if my mind went blank, he would tell me what to do. Throughout my circuit training, they both helped me enormously. I knew the training was having an effect as I pushed my trolley down the aisle of my local supermarket muttering, "November, November, downwind!" These words brought to mind the best hour of my week – when I was flying.

After Christmas I faced a second challenge at the flying club. This time it was social. I'd avoided the issue while I established myself in flying training, but as Christmas approached with its legacy of biting loneliness, I felt the need to branch out socially. I had spent almost every Saturday night at home for nearly three years. A notice appeared in the clubhouse advertising a series of lectures on Tuesday nights starting in the New Year and I decided to go along. It felt odd to travel along the country lanes in the dark on the first night, but when I arrived at Netherthorpe, the car park was half full. Determinedly, I walked through the door of the clubhouse and found myself the only woman amongst 20 men. One or two looked at me as I walked up to the bar and bought a cup of tea. Otherwise I was ignored and one part of me felt relieved. I chose a seat on my own near the window. No one spoke to me apart from a thin, dark haired man called Alan Grieve who came and sat nearby. A gentle man, he had already achieved what I was hoping for, his Private Pilot's Licence. The lecture began soon afterwards.

It was given by a tall, well-built man from the RAF called Sid Bowsher. I concentrated as he talked about the theory of flight but when he introduced a chart demonstrating the co-efficient of lift, my brain shut down. Alan whispered that he didn't understand it either. He had to go after the lecture ended and, with a friendly smile, took his leave. I slipped away, to escape the uncomfortable feeling of being one alone amongst the crowd.

The next two Tuesday evenings were the same, except that Alan didn't come again. I understood only part of the lectures, but found them useful because they were introducing new ideas that I would have to deal with as part of my training. On the social side, no one spoke to me and I didn't speak to anyone either. Part of me was frozen at the prospect of socialising. I was out of practice and the gruelling three years I had come through gave me no encouragement, yet there was part of me that wanted to.

On the fourth Tuesday, things changed. A grey haired man walked over to me before the lecture and introduced himself as Ray Carr. He was a student pilot as well and it was a relief to both of us to find somebody else at the same stage of training. At least there was now someone to talk to as we were both regular attenders at the lectures.

After that, a few people started to make casual conversation with me and the ice was broken. Then, one night towards the end of March, Sid Bowsher came and joined us after the lecture. He asked about my flying training and I told him I was struggling with the landing. He was very positive: "It often helps at this stage to book yourself ten lessons in a week. The concentrated practice should really push your flying along." It seemed a great idea to me, mainly because it meant flying twice a day every day for a week. I booked my lessons for the second week in April.

Four of them were cancelled due to the weather and four were productive in that I was making better landings – Ian actually took to folding his arms as I did the landing. I wasn't sure whether it was a discipline to stop himself grabbing the controls, or complete confidence. The other two lessons were less successful, mainly because I was mentally tired. However, I knew I was getting close to solo when Ian set about showing me what to do if my engine failed. Even a student on first solo has to be able to deal with that. We managed the emergency drill, but as I finished my last lesson on the Friday, I still had not gone solo. I knew Ian was as frustrated as I was with my variable performance.

I flew again six days later and was relieved to find that the undoubted improvement from the previous week wasn't lost. But still Ian wouldn't let me go solo and I wondered if it would ever happen.

Solo

The next day, Friday 21 April, had a strange feel to it. Ian telephoned me at 9.30 am and said, "Conditions are perfect – can you come in early?" Conditions for what? Minutes later I was belting my way to the airfield. The mystery continued when I arrived. Ian wasn't there at first and another instructor called Bob Sutherland, tall and grey, looked at me with an air of expectancy. He pointed through the large window to November November – "Go check it out" he said, as though he knew something I didn't. Then I heard Ian calling from the flight centre door – "How much fuel have we got?" "About two hours," I replied. "That should do it!" He grinned at me.

It was a good flying day and for the next hour we 'bashed' the circuit. I knew my landings were fine and then Ian concentrated on take-offs. They were fine too and, as we returned to the hold for circuit number six, I wondered what would happen next. Ian sat there with his arms folded. He looked at me directly and said, "I'm getting bored with this!" The moment had come. I panicked: "Stay with me for just one more!" Grudgingly he agreed, and this time he stayed silent and left me to it. Five minutes later we were back at the hold. "I'm getting really bored with this," said Ian. "Okay, I'll do it!" I growled back. He watched me through my final checks and gave me a long look before climbing out. "Good luck! I'll be in the tower. The aeroplane will feel lighter without me." He banged the door and was gone. This was it.

Taking a deep breath to calm my beating heart, I turned November November on to runway 24 and gave it full throttle. I remember thinking, "I could just pull the throttle and walk away," but I didn't. Seven seconds later I was airborne, aware that whatever else I might choose to do in my life I was committed to flying this circuit.

During the climb out towards Whitwell Woods I felt the aircraft drifting to the right and I heard Ian nagging me about it – only he wasn't there. And he was right, the aeroplane did climb better without his weight. I turned cross wind over the woods and levelled out with November November's nose on the base of the chimney in Whitwell. At the corner of the woods, I turned downwind and could see Steetley works ahead of me. Once in line with the end of the runway, I made the famous call for myself, "November November, downwind, 24 left." All the time, a flood of adrenalin kept me focused on the things I needed to do to stay safe. One of those things was a prayer to Cyril, "Just get me down safely!" I repeated it between my downwind checks. Then I heard Ian's voice calling to a visiting aircraft, "Aircraft calling Netherthorpe, there is circuit traffic, including a student on first solo!"

I turned November November onto base leg and set it up for the approach and landing. This was the part of the circuit where flying became a deadly serious business. This bit had to be right. I slowed the aeroplane down and put down the flaps. With a pounding heart I turned onto final and sought, successfully, to place the white concrete numbers in the right spot in the windscreen and to keep them there. I reckoned later I was concentrating so hard on the numbers that, if a nuclear missile had been shot through the back end of November November, I wouldn't have noticed.

The ground was coming up fast the way it does when you get down to the last 100 feet and touch down is only seconds away. I came over the hedge at the required 55 knots and glanced out of the side window and at the grass passing close by underneath. Then I gently raised the nose just as Ian had taught me and presented my wheels to the ground for one of the smoothest landings I had ever made. Ian's pleased voice came over the radio, "Good one, Sheila!" A swift release of pent up energy replaced the adrenalin, and fear, relief and euphoria were mixed up together. I knew I looked as though my face had been cut in half by the size of my smile – nothing had prepared me for the intensity of going solo. I managed to remember to take in the flaps and taxied back past the radio tower to the flight centre where Ian was standing waiting. As I reached the tower, I noticed that there was someone in the fire truck with the engine running. Bemused, I carried on and came to a halt close to the flight centre, where Ian signalled me into a parking spot. We looked wordlessly at each other through the aeroplane window. I did my final checks, shut down the engine and opened the door. Ian came round the end of the wing and I laughed out loud and shouted at him, "You old bugger!" He laughed back delightedly and gave me a kiss on the cheek. "Congratulations!"

The people in the flight centre must have thought I'd had a dose of laughing gas as I paid my bill. Then I said, "What's with the fire engine? Surely I wasn't that bad!" Ian answered my question as he came from the back of the flight centre "It's an RAF tradition that, when you go first solo, they get the fire truck out! If anyone thought you really needed it, you wouldn't be going solo. It's recognition of what you have achieved. And so is this!" He handed me a signed First Solo certificate, which I stared at for a long time and then placed carefully with my belongings. We shared a cup of tea and then it was time to go home.

To Be a Pilot

Loneliness closed in on me as I drove away from the airfield – on the best day of my flying career, there was no one to tell at home. I felt desolate as I bought a bottle of wine at my local off-licence and, when I reached home, I telephoned my closest friend, Pat Crooks.

"I've soloed today!" I burst out as soon as she answered. "Brilliant!" she said. I asked her, "Can I come round and celebrate tonight?" "Sheila, I'm so sorry, but we're going out." Sadness killed the conversation for me and I barely managed to say goodbye. It's one of the awful things about being on your own – everyone else has busy lives and you're only one among many. But to be alone on first solo day was obscene. I didn't think it could get any worse, but it did.

In an attempt to fill the void that afternoon, I went to a camera shop and bought a projector and screen for a slide show on the Himalayas that I was developing. I set the projector up in my lounge and switched it on. Within a few seconds, puffs of smoke were billowing out from the motor and little yellow flames leapt upwards. I switched it off and sat in Cyril's chair and cried my heart out. In the early evening I drank the bottle of wine and went to bed.

But the sun did come up next day and my friend, Jim Whittington, from the running club came and sorted out the projector. And I still had the personal satisfaction of now being a proper aviator, and it is that which is so special about first solo. An aviator can take an aeroplane out, fly it and bring it back safely, and I'd done it.

I remember thinking that going solo is like losing your virginity – it happens once and you never forget it. And second solo is like sex the second time – it's better. I flew solo for the second time two weeks later following a circuit session with Ian. It wasn't as exciting as the first, but the satisfaction was greater because the flying felt as though it belonged to me and that I was in charge of it.

I had a total of three hours solo to do in the circuit – the idea was to reinforce my circuit skills and build my confidence. With Ian and Martyn's help, I completed that by the end of June and then moved on to the next stage of training – navigation and cross-country. Flying cross-country required a new range of skills and I gained these at ground school, which took place in the flight centre. The first course I signed up for was radio-telephony as I had to have a radio licence to use the radio in the aeroplane; but the greatest benefit from the course was getting to know other students. Ray Carr, from the Tuesday night lectures, was on it, and so was Gordon Sherwin, an older student, who really broke the ice for us. One night when it was his turn to practise radio procedure from the next room where there was a second receiver, he was overcome by nerves and his voice dissolved into what soon became gales of hysterical laughter. Even when the instructor had suggested that he get some fresh air, we could still hear Gordon's wild giggles from the car park. We didn't learn much that night but the session in the bar afterwards was hilarious.

The clubhouse brought me other opportunities. By now, I was regarded as a flying nut – I would fly at every opportunity and said "Yes!" to anyone who invited me to go flying. I said "Yes!" to Wilf Haynes, a long-established club member, who invited me to France for lunch one Sunday towards the end of June. Wilf, a large man who enjoyed his food, was a flying nut in a more expensive kind of way – he'd owned different aeroplanes at different times in his life, sometimes having more than one at once, and he was happy to share his experience and knowledge with people who wanted to learn. Passport in my pocket, I drove to Gamston airfield, 10 miles east of Netherthorpe, and Wilf introduced me to his Rockwell Commander, November 4698 Whisky, a four-seater with a big engine. We flew to Southend where we landed, put on our life jackets for flying across the Channel, and Wilf filed a flight plan. The flight plan was important for safety – it alerted the authorities on both sides of the Channel that we would be crossing. If we were more than 30 minutes late, the Search and Rescue services would be called out. An hour after we took off, we landed in Le Touquet on the French coast and were on our way by taxi to the elegant sea front where we had lunch al fresco at a seaside restaurant. As I sat drinking a glass of lager in the sunshine and looking out to sea, I felt like a millionaire. But Wilf was determined to help with my flying in other ways. Several times he came and worked through my radio procedures with me in the flight centre and I could feel my confidence growing. I passed my radio test without any problems.

Alongside the radio course, I took a double course in navigation and meteorology. I enjoyed them because they were directly relevant to my stage of training. They were hard work – the navigation, although similar in principle to mountain navigation, required much more mathematics, and the meteorology demanded that I learn to read weather charts. Whenever I planned a flight, I used both these subjects. I also learned how to use the 'whizzy' wheel, or the manual computer, for working out flight times, wind drifts and headings. Unfortunately, what I learned was not what the instructor, a lieutenant from the RAF, tried to teach me. On the evening we were supposed to learn about the 'wind down' method of using the whizzy wheel, I had just returned from a splendid day at Brittas Bay in the Republic of Ireland to which I'd flown with two other club members. We arrived back at Netherthorpe at 7 pm and I climbed out of the club four-seater and went straight into the lesson in the flight centre. I was so tired after the long day that I struggled to keep my eyes open until, at last, my head fell forward and I was asleep. During that short time, Lieutenant X demonstrated the whizzy wheel. When he noticed my snores, he ended the lesson and gave us a sheet of problems for homework. I didn't understand a word of it. Next day, I found the words 'wind down' in my navigation book and I learned the 'wiggle' method. The following week Lieutenant X gave me a very odd look as I used it in class, but it worked for me.

Between ground school and flying training I was attending the airfield almost daily. There were two benefits from this – I was getting to know more people and the feelings of loneliness as I drove home stopped. I began to feel at home there and, as June came to an end, I decided to ask about part-time work in the flight centre. I reasoned that, if I was spending most of my time there, I might as well get paid for some of it. Part-time work became available at the end of July and from then on I combined it with finishing off my training.

What I loved most about working in the flight centre was the sound of the Lycoming engines in the Cessnas as they climbed away from runway 06, straight past the large window, often deafening me on the telephone. I loved being in an atmosphere where everything was to do with flying and I enjoyed the company of the instructors as they went about their daily work. I also learned what an airfield was like when the weather was bad – it was dead. Ian and Martyn had to attend at the airfield whatever the weather was like and they passed the time tormenting the office staff. On one occasion I was compelled to defend myself with a fire extinguisher when the two of them cornered me in the corridor of the flight centre and threatened to tickle me to death. They knew I would set it off if they didn't stop and they left me in peace. I had the feeling of coming out of a social desert and being able to have fun in male company. I was losing my sense of tragedy.

Sometimes my new life made me feel so cheerful that I felt guilty and I wondered what Cyril would have thought of it all. I suspected he would think I was crazy for working part-time for a pittance and for expending most of my time, energy and cash on something as impractical as flying. But mainly, I felt he would just want things to be all right for me whatever I was doing, and that he would have understood my need to be positive about life. Flying was certainly providing me with that.

I had three cross-country flights as a student – Ian referred to them as the 'small', the 'medium' and the 'big'. I did them dual first and then solo. Martyn supervised my first one which required me to fly west from the airfield to Junction 29 on the M1, just north of Mansfield, up the motorway to Junction 32, abeam Sheffield, and then back to the airfield. He lent me a map to flight plan it at home and I remember drawing the lines on it at my dining room table. It was a beautiful day and every time I looked up from the map through the window to the blue sky, I felt a connection between my inner and outer worlds. I made a successful solo flight the next day and had no worries about being out of sight of the airfield by myself for the first time.

Ian supervised the medium flight. It took me over Newark in Nottinghamshire, north along the River Trent to Gainsborough in Lincolnshire, and then back to Netherthorpe. I did the solo flight immediately after I had done the dual and Ian was satisfied. We then moved on to the big one which was important as it was the qualifier for my licence. Before I did it I had to pass my navigation flight test. This was to ensure I could cope with a diversion from a planned route. Ian set me to planning a triangular route from Netherthorpe to Skegness airfield and then on to Carnaby airfield, just south of Bridlington. We took off in November November mid-morning one day near the end of August 1995, four months after I had gone solo. I found my way to Skegness, but, as I tracked north to Carnaby and was approaching Covenham Reservoir, Ian announced that Carnaby was shut because of low cloud and we had to divert to Binbrook. So I had to find it on my air chart, estimate the heading to it from where we were, and fly to it. Ian said, "Get me there and you'll have passed." We flew in silence as I scanned the horizon. At last I saw a big concrete runway in the distance and four minutes later we were in the overhead. Ian looked at me and grinned, "You're through! Now take me back to Netherthorpe!"

The solo big cross-country took place on Saturday 23 September, and with the exception of first solo, it was the best part of my training. The flight was in three legs with away landings at Leicester and Peterborough Conington. I took off from Netherthorpe and flew south to Leicester airfield, which was operated by Leicester Flying Club. I managed to talk to East Midlands on the radio without drying up, and I joined the circuit at Leicester for a neat landing. Once parked, I made my way to the tower to have my cross-country form stamped – it confirmed that I had arrived safely and alone. An instructor signed it and, satisfied with a job going well, I headed for the stairs. Then I had one of those moments which are a landmark in flying training. As I walked down the stairs, one of the men in the tower came to the top and called, "Who was captain of the aircraft?" I hesitated only for a second before answering: "Dyson, Sheila Dyson!" I walked out of the tower with a swagger.

At Peterborough Conington my arrival was a different matter. I felt less sure of myself as I came into their overhead and joined the circuit and it showed in my tense landing – the Cessna's tyres squealed on the concrete runway. However, at least, we were down. I took my form to the tower where the man behind the desk showed no interest. Wordlessly he reached for a rubber stamp, banged it down on the form, scribbled an untidy signature on it and shoved it back at me. I managed to smother the rude comment that was about to leap out of my mouth, and five minutes later took off for the final leg back to Netherthorpe.

I'd been flying for two and a half hours by the time I landed and used the last of my mental energy to sort out the paperwork in Ian's office. I spent the rest of the afternoon lounging in one of the comfortable old leather armchairs in reception and told anyone who would listen what a great day it was. I was one step away from being a licensed pilot.

The final task was my General Flight Test where the examiner, Ian, tested me on all my basic skills. Although he was my main instructor, at that time it was accepted practice that he could also be examiner for my GFT. A few days after my qualifying cross-country we took off for a revision session. As we flew eastwards we climbed to 5,000 feet where I spent an hour practising steep turns and stalls. We returned to the airfield where I was delighted when Ian told me that the session was part of my GFT and I'd got through it. A second 'revision' session a few days later had a different result.

Again, we flew east and Ian took a critical look at my general aircraft handling and emergency procedures. We did this over Scofton, a disused airfield near Worksop. As we flew home, I had a feeling that this would become part of my GFT, but I nearly blew it. We had been flying for an hour when we reached Netherthorpe and I was expecting that we would land, but Ian directed me to do another circuit as he wanted to test another kind of approach and landing. Suddenly, I felt utterly weary and my concentration and quality of flying faded rapidly. Next thing Ian was shouting at me, berating my flying. My only thought was that if I had been in sole charge of the aeroplane, I would have landed as soon as possible. The pressure built up inside my head and suddenly, I yelled into the microphone, "Will you shut up!" Silence, blessed silence. I looked across at him warily. Tersely, he said, "If that's how you feel, we'd better land." "Yes," I said. It was a miserable end to the flight.

Back in the flight centre he disappeared into his office without a word and I stood miserably at the desk filling in my log book and thinking that, if the flight had been part of my GFT, I'd blown it. Lost in thought, I paid no attention to the sound of thunder outside. Boom! Boom! "There's an aeroplane down!"

Disbelieving, we watched as a low wing Trinidad aeroplane slid past the window on its belly. In a moment, the flight centre emptied as we raced across to where the Trinidad had ground to a halt. Disbelief struck again as the pilot stepped neatly out on to the wing, pulled out his mobile phone and, a moment later, was heard to say, "Darling, I don't think we'll be going to Belgium today!"

An engineer from Dukeries Aviation, the resident engineering company on the airfield, soon decided that, as only the undercarriage seemed to have been affected, the aeroplane could be manhandled off the runway to be parked outside the engineering hangar. As everyone worked and the pilot described what had happened, it became apparent that he had forgotten to put his undercarriage down. I was impressed by the communal effort to help him – it reminded me of the mountaineering tradition of helping a comrade in distress. There was another benefit from the incident – it gave Ian and me something to think about other than falling out over a GFT. Back in the flight centre I knocked on his office door and, moments later, apologised to him for my outburst, explaining how mentally tired I'd felt. He appreciated my honesty and signed off another part of my GFT in my log book. I also learned something from the incident – I could make flying decisions for myself. A week later we finished the test peacefully and my flying training was complete. I had only one ground school to finish and that was the technical exam. I surprised myself by passing that with relative ease. Then I filled in a large application form for my Private Pilot's Licence with Ian and sent it off to the Civil Aviation Authority. All I could do now was wait for the issue of my licence.

Two nights later I went to see my friend Pat, who had had to decline my invitation to celebrate on first solo day. As we lazed in her lounge drinking large vodkas, she asked me, "What would Cyril think now that you've finished your licence?" I said, "I can just see him up in heaven sitting on his cloud and puffing on his pipe. He'd be looking down on me and keeping an eye on me and he'd be just like he was when he was alive. I once told him I wanted to learn to fly and he said we couldn't afford it. Actually, we could have, but you don't think that at the time. And when I went for my first lessons, I could almost hear him say, 'What's she doing that for? I told her it was a waste of time!' But he'd know I'd carry on anyway and then he'd say, 'Who's that chuff taking her flying – he'd better look after her!'

"Then when I went solo I could see him watching me and he'd be pointing out to anyone else who passed by, 'That's my Sheila down there!' And he'd be as proud as punch. More than anything that's what he'd be. He was like that when he was alive – he'd be negative about something new I wanted to try and, then as I got on with it, he'd get interested and eventually end up telling everyone about it." At the thought of it, Pat and I burst out laughing.

My Private Pilot's Licence finally arrived on 9 November 1995. I watched as the young dark-haired postman, Aaron, walked down my drive. For the last week I'd been quizzing him whenever I'd seen him coming down the road. He knew what I was waiting for and, teasing, he held back the thick white envelope when I opened the door. "You have to sign for it!" he said, grinning. Then it was mine. I sat in Cyril's chair while I opened it and withdrew the little brown book that said I was a pilot. I kept looking at it, thinking how calm I felt in the moment of fulfilment of my second dream. Perhaps I was calm because my flying career wasn't ending at that moment, only beginning. Within two hours, I had bought a share in a small aeroplane.

G-AJIT

I fell in love with G-AJIT (registration Golf-Alpha Juliet India Tango) in the summer of 1995. One Saturday afternoon I watched a smart looking aeroplane being pushed out of the hangar at Netherthorpe and, from first sight, I thought it a handsome beast. Most people think of aeroplanes as female, but I always thought of G-AJIT as male.

G-AJIT was an Auster J1 and had the distinctive Auster shape, with broad high wings, a high maroon nose and propeller, big strong wheel struts and fat tyres. The long, cream fuselage tapered to a small tail wheel which was topped by a large rudder and tail plane. And he was in excellent condition for his 48 years. First registered in 1947, he had had a varied career as a training aircraft until being rescued as a derelict from the back of a hangar at Shobdon airfield in the early 1980s. The rebuild, carried out by enthusiasts, took over 12 years and when G-AJIT was finally completed in 1994, the G-AJIT group was formed. I was one of six co-owners. So, what prompted me to buy a share?

It was something I had read in a book called *A Gift of Wings*, a collection of articles written by an American, Richard Bach. One of the articles was entitled 'Why You Need an Aeroplane – and How to Get It'. When I started flying I had no intention of buying an aeroplane or a share in one – I couldn't afford it. By the time I'd read Bach's article, I'd decided I had to have it anyway.

The article resonated in my head. Bach asked the critical question – why should anyone need an aeroplane? His answer was that owning an aeroplane fulfils part of life's purpose. I thought of my own burning desire to fly. Apart from the trigger on the flight back from Manchester, why should I feel so strongly about it? The desire seemed to come from nowhere – there was nothing in my background to arouse it, yet it was there.

Bach believed that the desire to own an aeroplane was a reflection of a love of the sky and the people who fly. I understood the connection between owning an aeroplane and loving the sky – it meant I could get to where I wanted to be any time I chose. Bach also thought that a love of the sky reflected a love of life itself and of one's fellow man. I didn't understand this at first, but then I thought of the years I had spent in the mountains with Cyril. Our shared love of the outdoors drew us together and helped to form an endless bond. The scattering of Cyril's ashes from Robin Hood's Cave became a physical expression of that. Mountains and flying both lead up into the sky and it's where I want to be.

Bach also considered the way a person might acquire an aeroplane. The answer was simple – wait and look around. The aeroplane for me would present itself and I would know it. That is exactly how it happened with G-AJIT.

From midsummer through to autumn I looked around. Several small aeroplanes drifted into view and I considered them, but in my heart I knew I wanted G-AJIT. I was lucky enough to have two rides in him with one of the group members, an experienced instructor named Mike Watts. I realised that G-AJIT would be a testing aeroplane to learn to fly – the main challenge being to land him in a neat three-pointer and make sure he stayed on the ground. G-AJIT'S suspension included springy bungee cords, which meant that if there was any flying speed left when he touched down, he would bounce back into the air. It didn't matter to me. I bought my share when my new licence was two hours old.

All through the winter Mike Watts showed remarkable patience as he worked with me to master G-AJIT's take-off and landing. Bad weather slowed my already slow progress – the flying contrast between G-AJIT and November November was such that it made learning to fly G-AJIT like learning all over again. Spring had turned into early summer before solo day arrived on 27 May 1996.

The circumstances of this solo were very different from my first as a student. It took place in the evening, rather than at noon. I'd had a good circuit session with Mike and managed not to bounce any of the landings. We turned off the runway to taxi back to the hold for another circuit. Suddenly, Mike said, "Well, do you want to go?" "YES!"

He made me taxi past the tower when he climbed out – he didn't like walking. As he went, he muttered, "Don't break it!" I was alone at last with G-AJIT.

Calmly, I taxied to the hold for runway 06, did my final checks and turned on to the runway. I gave G-AJIT full throttle and he started to gather speed as fast as my heart did. Then we were airborne. I climbed ahead, turned crosswind over the landscaped tip next to Shireoaks village, and then downwind over Steetley Works. "G-IT, downwind, 06 right!" was my radio call in my first G-AJIT solo. I turned on to base leg over Whitwell woods and then with heart thudding, on to final approach to land. I could hear Mike's voice in my head about nose down, airspeed under control, over the hedge at 45 knots, power off, let it settle down, flare, ease the stick back, touch down, stick fully back against the seat, gently apply the brakes. I'd done it. "Thank you, G-AJIT!" Those words marked the beginning of my eccentric habit of talking to the aeroplane.

Elated, I taxied back to the hangar and saw Mike coming down the tower steps, smiling. He was probably as relieved as I was that I'd finally soloed. Between us, we pushed G-AJIT back into the hangar and I enjoyed the generous comments of several other taildragger pilots who kept their aeroplanes in the same hangar. I felt as though I'd joined an exclusive club. And then I celebrated. This time it was not the lonely affair of my first solo, but a satisfying hour in the company of the airfield groundswoman, Judith Howe, and her kindly parents. Judith lived with them in a rambling farmhouse on the downwind leg close to Steetly Works – every time I did a circuit on 06 or 24, I flew over it. That night when she opened the front door, I yelled, "I did it, I went solo in G-AJIT!" and she smiled with pleasure because she'd been following my efforts for months. Her father opened a bottle of sherry and I spent the next hour giving them the gory details of the flight.

One of the things I liked about G-AJIT was that he travelled slowly – the cruise speed was 80 knots and this gave me time to look out of the window and enjoy the view. It was like an aerial version of hill walking – slow movement and time to navigate and savour my surroundings. It made me want to make an extended journey by air and I did make one that summer with another G-AJIT group member, Richard Eaton. We flew up to the Isle of Mull off the west of Scotland

and landed on the grass runway at Glenforsa, right next to the sea. We even camped on the side of the runway. We landed on Skye and Tiree and overflew Coll which surprised me with its flat, stony surface. Bad weather forced us back to Netherthorpe but I knew I wanted to do more of this kind of flying. Then G-AJIT gave me adventures closer to home, often in the company of Martyn Webster.

At the time I went to work in the flight centre I'd enjoyed the company of both Ian and Martyn who were so instrumental to my pilot's licence and, once I had achieved it, there was a short period where I felt at a loss. I'd grown used to having their backup and company when I flew and it took a while to detach from the instructor/student relationship. Martyn helped with this the day I turned up at the flight centre waving my new licence. I'd booked to fly a club aircraft and he volunteered to be my first passenger. Most pilots find it unnerving the first few times they fly when they carry full responsibility for the flight. And although I was ready for my licence, I had feelings of regret that I was no longer flying with Ian. We had come such a long way from my early lessons and I certainly wouldn't forget that it was he who sent me solo.

At the beginning of 1997 Martyn and I started cycling together on Saturday mornings, mainly because I asked if we could. I had to reduce the running that I did as my knees were giving trouble and I wanted an alternative way of keeping fit. Martyn belonged to a cycling club but he also seemed happy to cycle with me. Before long, we were going out together and it was wonderful to be able to share activities with a like minded individual, especially one so kind as Martyn. He became a

G-AJIT fan and we often flew in the summer evenings out over the Peak District where we had also started hill walking together on our days off. It felt so good to be close to someone again and know I could rely on him. Unfortunately, he wasn't with me one November day when I took off in G-AJIT for a farm strip at South Scarle, near Newark in Nottinghamshire.

I had developed an interest in farm strip flying which even on a good day provides a challenge. Often the approaches are awkward and the runways short. The runways are often in the middle of a field of crops with a hangar to the side or at one end, in which the farmer flyer keeps his aeroplane. Farmer flyers are invariably pilots with a strong sense of individuality who prefer the independence of having their own place to fly from. I enjoyed visiting them and I was riding high, gaining confidence and experience; but both Ian and Martyn warned me continuously about the fine line between confidence and complacency.

Before I took off, I telephoned Phil Clements who owned the strip at South Scarle. He said he'd be expecting me. Excited, I planned my route, but Martyn gave me yet another warning. He said, "It's an awkward strip. I suggest you fly first to the village of Collingham, about three miles north of Newark, and then left along the railway track just beyond it. You'll spot the strip because it's got an east-west runway and ends up against the railway line. Watch out for any trains – you don't want to hit one or give the driver a heart attack!"

I took off in G-AJIT and flew to Collingham on the east side of the River Trent. It was a fine, clear day and I spotted the railway line but, instead of turning left along it, I caused a problem for myself by crossing it, so having to approach from the opposite direction to that which Martyn had described. I flew along the railway line looking for a grass strip ending up against it with a large green hangar half way down it. I growled to G-AJIT, "Where the hell is it?"

Then I spotted a strip of green that ran up against the railway line. The crops on either side had been harvested and near the railway line, just off the green strip, was a building. Instinctively, I flew towards it – it wasn't the instinct that I'd found it, but rather that I would like to be safely back on the ground. I did a precautionary circuit at 300 feet to inspect the surface which looked green and level to me. The building to the side of the runway didn't look like a hangar, but I persuaded myself that it was a barn hangar where Phil Clements kept his aeroplane. And the green strip did end up against the railway line. I climbed away, flew a tight circuit and came in to land towards it. The confidence of my recent G-AJIT flying was there in a smooth approach with the airspeed under control – I would stop well before the small railway embankment at the end.

I knew it would be a good landing. Then, 10 feet off the ground, I realised that the green I was descending into wasn't grass. "Oh, shit!" I said to G-AJIT. Then I heard a voice in my head, "Stay with it!" I knew instantly that to try and go round would probably result in my hitting the embankment. I was committed, and a few seconds later landed comfortably on the soft, leaf-covered earth surface of a recently harvested sugar beet field. "Shit!" I kept saying to G-AJIT as I taxied along the runway to the building at the end. I parked facing the embankment and, feeling very stupid, climbed out and stood looking at the aeroplane.

Slowly, I walked all the way round it. Everything seemed normal, apart from green leaves and mud that were clogging the tail wheel. Then I looked down the length of my sugar beet runway. Would it be long enough for G-AJIT to take off? I badly needed to talk to someone about it. So, dressed in my green flying suit and feeling inexpressibly foolish, I knocked on the door of the farmhouse that I'd thought was a barn hangar. A middle-aged woman with a pleasant face opened the door. I spoke first: "I'm sorry to trouble you, but I've just landed in your field. May I use your telephone?"

She didn't bat an eyelid. "Yes, come in!" She gestured to her husband in the big, warm, untidy kitchen and continued, "I said to him, there's one landed in the field. We heard you go over the first time!" I explained that I'd been aiming for a farm strip nearby. I said, "I don't suppose you get many aeroplanes landing in your field on a Tuesday afternoon!" "Actually," she replied, trying not to laugh, "We don't own the field. Here's the phone. Would you like a cup of tea?" I telephoned Phil Clements and his response was immediate: "I know where you are, I'll be there in ten minutes." Something in his voice was immeasurably reassuring.

I was standing forlornly by G-AJIT when Phil's dirty green Range Rover pulled up at the gate and I watched him climb out. We met in the garden behind the farmhouse and the reassurance promised in the phone call became a reality. Phil walked across to me, put his arms around me in a great bear hug and kissed me soundly on the mouth.

Whatever is needed to solve the technical difficulties of getting an aeroplane out of a sugar beet field, when you're in the shit, nothing beats a bear hug and a smacker. In an instant, Phil Clements was my friend. In his sixties, he was wearing dirty overalls with a scruffy peaked cap on his head. He was strongly built with the physique of a man who had worked outdoors all his life. His face was tanned and whiskery and his voice deep, hard and clear – a man to have on your side and, on that day, he was certainly on mine.

He agreed with my suggestion that I should be able to take G-AJIT off the sugar beet runway by the hawthorn hedge at the end. We turned the aeroplane so that he faced away from the railway track but as close to the embankment as possible to give me the longest take-off run available. As we pushed G-AJIT back over the soft earth, he felt heavy as lead as Phil struggled to lift the tail and I struggled to push on the wing strut. Once G-AJIT was in position, we paced the length of the 'runway'. It was about 300 yards. Halfway along it there was a large bush and Phil advised me, "Get the tail up as soon as you can or the soft soil will slow you down. If your airspeed isn't up to at least half of lift-off speed by the bush, abort! You'll soon slow down."

I fired up G-AJIT's engine and, with full throttle and tail high, we charged down the runway. It was a slow charge. My eyes flicked from the airspeed indicator to the bush on the side of the runway and, as I neared it, instinct made me close the throttle. The airspeed was barely halfway to lift-off speed. I taxied back to where Phil was waiting, "That looked good," he said. "I really thought you'd make it."

Twice more I tried and twice more I closed the throttle as I came near the bush. By this time, I was at the limits of my confidence. I walked back to where Phil was standing. He took one look at me and said, "Best quit while everything's all right. You and the aeroplane are safe. Leave it for today. Come back to Beeches Farm with me and you can telephone Netherthorpe from there." I thanked the couple in the farmhouse for their kindness and they started laughing again. Better that than anger, I thought.

Phil contacted the farmer who owned the sugar beet field and he seemed to accept with good grace the unexpected presence of an aeroplane on his land. At Beeches Farm Phil made me a cup of tea while I contacted Martyn at Netherthorpe. He said, alarmed, "Are you all right? I had the feeling something was wrong." Subdued, I told him what had happened but, true to form, all I got from Martyn was kindness. I put him on to Phil and they made arrangements for G-AJIT's rescue the following day – I knew Ian would be able to fly G-AJIT out. As Phil drove me back to Nethethorpe, an hour's drive, he told me how his flying career almost came to end following an accident in which he'd lost an eye. I had a sense of his struggle to regain his flying licence and I ended up telling him about Cyril and my three dreams. He said little but I had the feeling that he understood a lot. Next day, Martyn and Ian rescued G-AJIT.

As the summer of 1997 approached, I started thinking about another distance journey in G-AJIT and when I suggested to Martyn that we make a flying and camping trip to Ireland, he agreed. We set off in mid-July with tent, sleeping bags and stove behind G-AJIT's seat. Martyn flew the first leg to Caernarfon where we re-fuelled, filed a flight plan and put on our life jackets. The next leg across the Irish Sea was mine – all 60 miles of it to the east coast of Ireland. The hazard of flying over the sea in a single-engined aeroplane has an added spice which made my spine tingle as I lined up on 26 for take-off.

Within five minutes, Anglesey disappeared beneath us and the horizon ahead was empty. All we could see from our 4,000 feet altitude was the deep blue sea showing tiny ripples. Above us was high cloud partially covering a blue sky. In turn, I had a strong sense of isolation, space, freedom and peace.

As we continued on our heading for a navigation beacon south of Dublin, we strained our eyes to see the Irish coast. At last, it came into view – a long, low, dark line on the horizon. Martyn was working the radio to Dublin Air Traffic Control: "Dublin, G-AJIT is VFR (flying visually) and requests special clearance to enter your airspace." Back came the reply, in a light Dublin accent: "G-AJIT, you are clear to enter Dublin airspace. We will bring you in visually." Two minutes later, Dublin ATC spoke again, "G-IT, can you see two large chimneys at the mouth of the river? Go to that point and report overhead."

I had a sense of wonder – here I was in a small aeroplane, my own, even though I shared it with five other people, in international airspace, on the edge of a major city and ATC was talking to us as if giving directions to the local bus stop. And the city was my city, where, for years, I had dreamed of becoming a pilot. Dublin ATC came on the radio again: "G-IT, follow the river, not above 1,500 feet." I could have kissed the ATC man as G-AJIT carried us along the River Liffey with its many bridges right into the heart of Dublin. This was a homecoming and a half. I said to Martyn in a broken voice: "If my mother was alive, she'd be tickled pink!" We followed the curve of the river into the gentle hills west of Dublin and soon saw the tarmac runway of Weston Airfield on the right. G-AJIT and I finished with a good landing and my first overseas flight as pilot in command was accomplished.

Martyn and I stayed overnight in a hotel in Dun Laoghaire and next morning visited my aunt Tesa Phelan in Monkstown. She was my Irish mother's only surviving sister and someone I admired deeply. She'd survived severe traumas in her life and yet was full of spirit with a generous heart. I saw something of her in myself in the way she dealt with things – sometimes shouting the odds, sometimes subdued, sometimes with a wonderful 'to hell with it' attitude. She made us welcome in her comfortable apartment and even took me to the local chemist where she bought me some disposable knickers and a new toothbrush – I'd left my clothes bag behind the hangar at Netherthorpe. So, duly re-equipped, Martyn and I set off on the next stage of the journey.

At Weston we filed a flight plan for Galway on the west coast. The flight took us across the central plain of Ireland, a flat, featureless area of extensive peat bogs. Fortunately, the visibility was good and we arrived safely at Galway. That night we camped at Salthill, on the outskirts of the city, and Martyn fell in love with Ireland. He loved the simplicity of camping and fresh air and of demolishing large glasses of Guinness and not waking up with a hangover.

Next day we flew on to Kerry airport near Killarney. I had to ask Kerry ATC, a man with a rich Kerry accent to repeat his instructions, but soon we were down and taxiing to the part of the airport where Kerry Flying Club had its base. That night we camped in a small enclosed field near the centre of Killarney. It was a balmy evening and after three hours of good food and Guinness, Martyn became even more enamoured of all things Irish. He started talking about going to work in Ireland as a flying instructor. I reached my high point of relaxation next morning after we telephoned for a taxi back to the airport. We sat on our bags on the pavement outside the telephone box eating a Magnum choc ice, enjoying the warmth of the sun. Sadly, the mood didn't last.

At the airport the forecast gave bad weather coming in from the west in two days time and we made the reluctant decision to start the journey home. We took off from Kerry for Kilkenny on the east side of Ireland, but made a major detour around the Ring of Kerry so that Martyn could see the rugged coastline with its endless cliffs and the waves crashing at their feet. The pale sun gleamed on the surface on the sea and inland, Carrantouhil, the highest mountain in Ireland raised its ramparts above the lakes of Killarney. We finished our circular journey over Killarney town and waved it a sad goodbye before flying east.

Kilkenny Airfield was a pleasant surprise after the tarmac runways of Galway and Kerry – there was 900 yards of grass with a slight incline. We refuelled G-AJIT for the flight to Weston the following morning and took a taxi to a campsite in the middle of the town. I felt a darkness coming over me – the kind that used to hit me whenever

Cyril and I returned from a camping and walking holiday on the Isle of Arran off the west of Scotland. I hate leaving places where I have been happy.

We reached Weston at lunchtime next day and, with the bad weather following us, made the decision to fly back to Caernarfon that afternoon rather than be trapped in Weston. Even the weather was gloomy as we approached Anglesey. Just as we landed at Caernarfon it caught us up and we were holed up there for the next two days. We had a superb evening flight back to Netherthorpe along the north Wales coast where the air was clear and smooth. There was a stiff crosswind at Netherthorpe when we arrived and Martyn suggested we divert to Sturgate, near Gainsborough, for a runway more into wind. But the urge to be home was strong and I decided to land at Netherthorpe. It was hard to keep G-AJIT on track and Martyn gave me a well-deserved lecture as we pushed the aeroplane back into the hangar.

As well as having much pleasure flying G-AJIT, I also learned a great deal. From the sugar beet field incident I learned the valuable navigation lesson of not making the ground fit the map. I learned also that there are great people in flying and that I knew three of them. The practical help and kindness of Phil Clements, and the flying skill of Ian and the risk he took on G-AJIT's and my behalf – the memories and friendships are precious still today. But most important of all was the relationship with Martyn, which extended well beyond the world of flying. And although we eventually went our separate ways, we still have an enduring friendship, based on a love of flying and the simplicity of the outdoors.

I worked in the flight centre from July 1995 until November 1997 and flying filled most of my waking hours. Between working in the office, flying itself and enjoying an active social life, my life in Sheffield was full. I continued my other activities such as fell running and hill walking, but flying was the dominant element and, when anyone asked me where I worked, I loved to be able to say, "On an airfield!" But as time passed, I began to feel overwhelmed by the intensity of the flying environment where there is a massive concentration on one activity. I felt the need to be away from it, to develop my life outside flying and the weekly visits to the Peak District took on a new importance. It was a question of balance, of enjoying a variety of interests rather than devoting myself exclusively to any particular one. Inevitably the time came to move on.

Something else had occurred during this period and it pulled together the threads of the previous four years. The occurrence was the fulfilment of my third dream, that of making a journey on the ice cap of Antarctica.

PART THREE

Antarctica

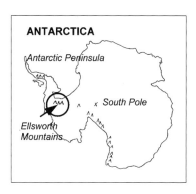

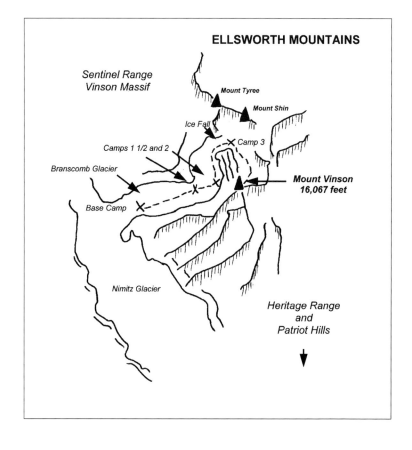

Decision

Inertia nearly killed Antarctica. I had to fight to keep the dream alive, in contrast to the urgency and drive of the first two. At the beginning of 1996 I knew I had to take action to fulfil it or I would lose it. Almost grudgingly, I started to make enquiries about getting on to the ice cap.

I learned that the only company to take private expeditions on to the ice were Adventure Network International (ANI) who at that time were based at Beaconsfield in Buckinghamshire. After months of discussion, I signed up for an expedition to climb Mount Vinson, 16,067 feet and the highest mountain on the continent. It is located in the Sentinel Range of the Ellsworth Mountains, some 700 nautical miles from the South Pole. I also arranged that after the expedition I would spend an extra ten days on the ice at the ANI Base Camp at Patriot Hills, simply to experience living on the ice. As in the Himalayas, I wanted to know more about the place beyond climbing the mountain. I found the decision to sign up agonising. Not only did I have a full, comfortable life in Sheffield, but I had to face my old fear of long journeys thousands of miles from home. Yet no matter how I tried to resist by putting up barriers, each was knocked down and the dream became a challenge that some inner part of me would not let go of. The only answer, ultimately, was to face it.

One barrier was a serious heart problem for my mother. She started to suffer from heart failure in March that year and I felt I could not possibly leave her if she was in any danger. She confounded my fears by being put on the 'fast track' for medical treatment and getting herself discharged from hospital in April. Another barrier was my knees, damaged and worn after years of hill walking and running. That barrier was knocked down by a visit to my home by an ANI mountain guide called Mike Sharp who lived near Sheffield. The office had phoned to say he would be in Sheffield and would be happy to call. I was so glad that he did. Tall and bearded, he had an outdoor quality with which I was familiar and, when he looked at the photograph on the lounge wall of me on the summit of Mera Peak and said, "You can do Mount Vinson!", my mind started racing. I told him about my knee problems and his answer was positive: "I had knee problems but there was a skiing trip I badly wanted to do, so I got over it! You can do the same!" And that's how it happened. I treated my knees gently for the next two months and in August, a few weeks before I had to make a final decision, I spent four days out in the Peak District walking with a heavy backpack up every steep hill I could find. I walked 34 miles with 8,000 feet of ascent and descent. At the end of it, my knees were fine.

The final barrier was the cost. ANI used aircraft as their mode of transport to, and on, Antarctica and aviation fuel was expensive. Consequently, costs were high. I spent weeks of sleepless nights – the cost would make serious inroads into my funds and I wasn't sure I was justified in doing this for one short period of my life. In the end, I justified it as my 'pearl of great price' – like buying my share in G-AJIT, I couldn't afford not to do it. Then, just when I had made up my mind to go ahead, no one would insure me. I could not afford to risk the sum involved. In desperation, I contacted Anne Kershaw, who ran ANI, and explained my predicament. Anne knocked this barrier down in one sentence: "Sheila, if anything prevents you from getting on the Hercules aircraft in Punta Arenas, you will get a full refund!" Her answer confirmed my first impressions of her, gained from a telephone call of two months before. She had contacted me at home to enquire if I had made a decision about the trip. When I told her about my mother's heart condition and the state of my knees, she listened and placed no pressure on me for a decision. I would contact her when I was ready. But that wasn't the end of the conversation. She was easy to talk to and I found myself telling her about Cyril being a mountaineer, his death, and the three dreams, including the fact that I was now a pilot. I came off the telephone with the feeling that Anne Kershaw understood exactly what I was talking about. So, very soon after she resolved my insurance problem, I committed myself to an expedition for January 1997, the latter end of the Antarctic summer. I would leave England on 30 December 1996 and spent the last four months of the year in hectic preparation.

Fitness was my first priority. I went to see Jon Tinker, one of the directors of Out There Trekking, the company which had taken me to the Himalayas. They were based at Woodseats, four miles from where I lived in Sheffield. Jon had successfully led one of the first commercial British expedition to Mount Everest. I asked his advice on training for a big mountain. His reply was short: "The best preparation for walking is walking! Plenty of walking with a big pack on your back. Fill it with water which you can empty out on the top of the hill and save your knees coming down. Use ski poles to help as well." I took his advice and, by mid-December, the weight had dropped off and I felt remarkably fit. I had gone out at least twice a week and walked many splendid routes in the Peak District. Then my knees started to object to the strenuous training and I was advised by Jim Mersch, a sports physiotherapist, to stop training or I would never get to Antarctica. With his help I recovered in time for my departure. The fitness I'd acquired over the previous four months would not be lost in two weeks.

The second priority was equipment. ANI sent me a detailed list of expedition gear and I felt a childish excitement as I started to acquire the items on it. I love getting presents and each night, as I watched TV in my lounge, I looked with pleasure at these presents to myself. They had special meaning for me as they were to be potential life-saving items on my greatest mountain journey.

One of the most important items was my sleeping bag which had to be proofed to –40 degrees Celsius. I took an old down bag of Cyril's to Rab Carrington's factory in Sheffield and he said he could alter it to meet my requirements. A few weeks later I collected a fat blue bag which was warm enough to melt the ice. It gave me a warmth of a different kind when I thought of its connection to Cyril – I would be carrying a part of him with me to Antarctica.

Two local outdoor companies helped me with the rest of my gear. One of them was Foothills, an outdoor shop in Sheffield. Ian Brown, nicknamed Hovis, who had known Cyril from years before, supplied me with many general items, while Outside, a shop in Hathersage which specialised in expedition gear, supplied me with my footwear and down clothing. The royal blue down jacket and salopettes made me look like a Michelin woman and I was amazed to find that I needed size

11 boots to fit in the extra layers around my feet. There were seven layers between them and the ice. They included thermal socks; vapour barrier socks to stop any moisture around my feet from freezing; two pairs of thick, woollen expedition socks; foam-lined inner boots; thick-soled outer plastic boots; neoprene over boots; and beyond all of these were my crampons.

All my clothing was thermal, even down to my bra and pants. Over them I wore a heavy duty thermal vest and long johns and a woollen sweater. I topped them off with 'Buffalo' salopettes and top with a detachable hood. The Buffalo items had a fleece lining and a windproof outer perlon layer. Head gear included a thermal balaclava and a neoprene face mask which looked like the yashmak worn by Muslim women, to protect my face against frostbite. My hands were protected by thin, thermal gloves, windblock gloves and a huge pair of insulated climbing mittens. By the time I had acquired all my gear and clothing, my lounge resembled the storeroom of an outdoor centre.

The last thing I had to deal with was my travel arrangements and any apprehension I felt about travelling to the bottom end of South America was soon dispelled by the professional reassurance of Wild Wings, who arranged my flights. I was to travel to Punta Arenas via Madrid, Recife in Brazil and Santiago in Chile. I looked forward to the flight over the Andes. The preparations were completed just before Christmas and all that was left to do was to stuff all the gear into my big rucksack and the large German army kit bag which I'd bought. I also had to say goodbye to my mother.

Since Cyril died we had become very close. Each of us, in the other, had a direct link to Cyril and it brought much comfort to us both. I loved sitting with her in her homely kitchen where we would sort out the world's problems. She had great awareness of current political issues and could debate them as well or better than any politician. Inherently shy, she had been thrust into the local limelight in 1970 when she became Lady Mayoress of the City of Sheffield for her husband Sydney Dyson, who had been elected as Lord Mayor. His career had been that of political agent for two Labour Members of Parliament and Mary had been unwillingly drawn into it. She supported Sydney wholeheartedly until his death in 1978 but then took her chance to pursue her own career in art. She has considerable talent and is very productive. Her kitchen – she calls it her 'Art Gallery' – is filled with water colours and decoupaged pictures of her own making.

She spent Christmas with me as usual and we got on well together but were both aware of the big break to come. I was restless to be going and she was sad. Tactfully, she suggested she would go home early and it was better for both of us. When I went to see her to make my final farewell, I sensed her deep sadness. She told me to be careful and I told her not to worry – we both knew the other would do the opposite. Leaving her was my only regret as I headed south.

Getting There

The weather forecast for Sunday 30 December was atrocious. Blizzard conditions were predicted right across the United Kingdom and I decided to travel from Sheffield to London Heathrow, my departure airport, a day early. It was as well that I did, as the foul weather arrived as forecast and Britain was covered in snow for the next three weeks.

I spent the night in a freezing hotel room near the airport – the central heating had failed. It was like the final stage of training for Antarctica. Next morning after check-in I took a seat in the departure lounge to wait and my mind drifted to the little brown bear that my friend, Pat, had given me to take on the journey. I'd named him Elmer after a snowman I'd built in the back garden with Cyril one January afternoon several years before. Elmer was now stowed in my small blue and black rucksack, the same one in which I'd carried Cyril's ashes to Robin Hood's cave and that I'd used on the ascent of Mera Peak – I couldn't separate Cyril from my dreams. We boarded the aeroplane and, even as we taxied to the hold for take-off, snow flakes fluttered past the windows.

At Madrid I found the Lan Chile desk and checked in my luggage for the flight to Recife and Santiago. The flight originated in Frankfurt which was also experiencing severe weather conditions and there was a delay: we finally took off for Santiago at 2.40 am. I slept for three hours and woke to see the sun rise – a huge red ball that stretched its beams over layers and lumps of cloud. After refuelling in Recife on the east coast of Brazil I watched forests and swamps passing below us before I fell asleep again. We landed in Santiago mid-afternoon local time.

The final flight was to Punta Arenas at the southern end of Chile and we flew at 35,000 feet over the Andes. I watched as the foothills gave way to volcanoes of increasing height. Most were covered with glaciers and some had snow-covered cones. In the high Andes, broad glaciers flowed downhill from the summits, often pushing through deep valleys. At Punta Arenas airport I was welcomed by Anne Kershaw of ANI and her colleague, Lesley. I could hardly keep my eyes open as we drove to Hotel Condor de Plata where I was staying. I didn't care that it was New Year's Eve – I fell into bed and was asleep in seconds.

I woke next morning to a new year on a new continent. After breakfast, I went out to explore. Most of the streets in Punta Arenas sloped downhill to the sea and I followed Colon Avenue down to the beach where the vivid blue sea was being whipped by a brisk wind into white-topped waves. There were few people about – probably like people in Sheffield, most were in bed with a headache. I looked across the Straits of Magellan, a kind of inland sea that separates Chile from Tierra del Fuego. I walked across the soft, dark brown sand and put my hand in the cold water that came from the Southern Ocean, where Antarctica was.

After lunch I went to the ANI office in Arauco where a cheerful young Englishwoman called Faye, Anne Kershaw's personal assistant, took me around the office and then into the radio room where I met Steve, the English radio operator, and his Chilean wife, Mariella. Steve had previously worked for the British Antarctic Survey but, however long he'd been away from home, he couldn't hide his pleasant Wiltshire accent. As I left, Faye told me my kit would be inspected the following morning and there would be a briefing at Hotel Cabos des Hornos in the evening, when I would meet my fellow travellers.

Next morning I underwent a thorough kit inspection by Sue, a New Zealand member of the ANI staff. When she'd gone, I repacked my gear, keeping out the things that I would need for my arrival on the ice at Patriot Hills, including plastic snow boots, crampons, windproofs, gloves and my orange balaclava. The last was my longest standing item of mountain wear. A friend had given it to me for Christmas in 1975 and it had been everywhere with me ever since, including the Canadian Rockies, the Swiss Alps, Iceland, the Himalayas and all over the British Isles. If I reached the summit of Mount Vinson, it would be there as well. Sue collected my luggage that afternoon.

Cabos des Hornos was one of the best hotels in the city. In the early evening, I walked through the huge marble foyer into the smart bar where I ordered a beer while I waited for the briefing to start. Most people go down to Antarctica in ships but ANI had found another way of getting on to the ice and that was in a Hercules aircraft. The briefing was to prepare us for this.

The conference room filled rapidly with ANI staff and clients and the aircrew of the Hercules. I didn't know anyone apart from the staff so I took the plunge and placed myself next to the toughest looking man in the room. With a grey, shaven head and whiskery face, he turned out to be a cameraman from a Croatian television crew who were making a series about a team of Croatian and Slovenian climbers who were doing the Seven Summits Challenge. In it climbers have to reach the summit of the highest mountain on each of the seven continents. The cameraman soon became bored with me and walked away. Next I spoke to an American mountain guide called Skip Horner who was using ANI facilities to take a group of climbers to Mount Vinson. Once there, his group would be self-sufficient.

The meeting was opened by Anne Kershaw who gave an excellent slide presentation on Antarctica. Of slender build, with a striking face and long blond hair, she held the rapt attention of the mainly male audience – some because she was their employer, and the rest because her words and slides conveyed the startling beauty of Antarctica, especially the shots of the Transantarctic Mountains whose sharp rocky summits penetrated the ice cap and rose like rockets to the sky. It was an audience that needed no convincing. Her final words brought the immediacy of Antarctica home to each of us: "When you get on the Hercules, make sure you have your down gear with you. You'll take off in pleasant temperatures in Punta Arenas but when you step on to the ice at Patriot Hills, it will be very cold. Bring your snow boots with you and your hat and gloves. Also, take care when you're walking from the aircraft to the camp – it's been known for an expedition to end because of a sprained ankle just after someone got off the aeroplane."

The briefing was followed by a piscol cocktail party. After several glasses of it – a mixture of egg whites, sugar, piscol and Grant's whisky – I found myself in conversation with Sue, the inspector of my gear. The piscol couldn't stop the tension rising in me when she said,

"You're the only person left on your expedition. The other two pulled out two weeks ago!" Stunned, I found Anne and said, "Is there something I should know about?" She laughed at first and then said seriously, "This will work out well for you because you'll have Dave Hahn to yourself. The expedition will be tailored to suit you. He's an excellent guide, laid back but very professional. He's a kind man and will do everything he can to help you." I believed her, liked the sound of him and started to feel curious to meet him. Not long afterwards, I walked unsteadily back to Hotel Condor de Plata where I fell into bed – we had been instructed to arrange an early call for a 6 am departure to Antarctica. Drunk or not, I didn't sleep a wink.

Sleep did come after my early morning call to ANI when I learned the flight had been delayed, but an urgent call from Lesley at 11 am jerked me into action. The minibus for the airport would collect me at noon. I made a farewell call to my mother in Sheffield. When she answered and heard my voice, she said, "What's up?" "I'm off to Antarctica today!" I said and could hardly believe my own words.

On the minibus I found myself squashed next to Sue who impressed me with the information that, when she wasn't working for ANI, she ran an English language school in Bolivia – a tough proposition for anyone. Lesley collected our passports once we arrived at the airport and soon we were allowed on to the apron where the Hercules was parked and waiting. I couldn't take my eyes off it.

The length of the fuselage was shorter than most airliners, but it was also deeper and broader. Its high wings were heavily laden with the weight of four turbo-prop engines and two fuel pods. Under the high tail plane the fuselage flattened out to provide a broad ramp, now lowered to accept the piles of luggage and supplies waiting on the tarmac. The cockpit was high above the ground with square windows just as I'd seen on a Lancaster bomber. The main wheels were placed near the rear of the fuselage and were almost in line with its belly, no doubt to give the aircraft a low centre of gravity. The nose wheel was to the rear of the cockpit area. The ANI logo was painted along the white and grey fuselage, while the SAFAIR logo was painted on the tail fin – the latter being the South African company from whom the aeroplane was chartered. The two companies played a vital part in the history and current activities of Antarctica.

Aviation announced its arrival down there with the first flight over the South Pole on 29 November 1929. Richard Bird, an American, mounted the expedition and flew as navigator to Bernt Balchen, the pilot. In the mid-1980s aviation merged with mountaineering and triggered the establishment of Adventure Network International.

The company was founded by Giles Kershaw, Anne's husband, and two colleagues. In 1985 he flew two Canadians, Pat Morrow and Martyn Williams, on to the Branscomb Glacier, close to the Vinson Massif. They were on the Antarctic leg of the Seven Summits Challenge. Giles used a Twin Otter aircraft for the journey and realised he had solved some of the logistical problems of transporting people on to different parts of the continent. He made a major breakthrough the following year when his colleague Jim Smith landed a DC-4 on the ice runway at Patriot Hills. After that, ANI became the sole organisation that had regular flights on to the ice. They started using the Hercules in

1993 and it was held in awe by those who flew in it, either as pilot or passenger. Landing on the ice promised an interesting arrival – the civilian Hercules was not licensed to use skis and we would be landing on rubber tyres.

Once the ramp had been raised and doors locked, I sat next to an American climber near the back of the airline seats that filled half the fuselage. The overweight climber had little to say and, as he settled in his seat, I noticed his jacket parting company with his trousers to expose bare flesh just above his buttocks. I had a feeling he'd be cold in Antarctica. As the pilot fired up the four engines, I took a good look round the inside of the Hercules. It was like a large cavern. Along the walls were endless rows of control cables, electric wires and pipes. As the engines throbbed in readiness, the airframe vibrated and I noticed a distinctive smell – a mixture of oil, jet fuel and the mechanical and human smells that permeate every aeroplane. I sat there and sniffed the air like a glue sniffer. We lifted off five minutes later and were soon lost in the cloud that covered Punta Arenas and the Straits of Magellan.

An hour into the flight I undid my seat belt and, having checked it was all right with Anne who was busy making sandwiches at the back of the cabin, I climbed the spiral metal stairs to the flight deck. It was large and cramped with four seats – two for the captain and co-pilot and two for the engineer and technician on duty. There were two bunks at the back for the off duty crew. Forward of the pilots' seats was a large instrument panel and the windscreen. Through it, I watched Drake's Passage slipping under us. The sky was clean and blue apart from small puffs of white cloud. Below us, the sea reflected the deep blue of the sky. I learned from the instruments that we were at 21,000 feet and doing 300 knots.

On my third visit to the flight deck, I finally saw Antarctica. Rising abruptly out of the sea was an ice cliff that extended right across our view. It was the coast of Alexander Island, close to the edge of the continent but almost permanently joined to it because of the pack ice that fills the narrow channel between the two. To the left of the island, the Antarctic Peninsula stretched away 1,100 miles to the north. Minutes later, the Hercules carried us over the edge of the continent and we continued south towards the Ellsworth Mountains which were named after Lincoln Ellsworth, an American who made the first trans-Antarctic flight on 22 November 1935. Mount Vinson was named after an American Congressman, Carl Vinson, who did much to promote Antarctic exploration during the period 1935-1961. Within the Ellsworth range, there are many smaller ranges. The one containing Mount Vinson, the Sentinel Range, is separated from the Heritage Range by the Nimitz Glacier and alongside these are located Patriot Hills, where the ice runway is. Once past the glacier, the Hercules started its descent and tension mounted in the cabin. I imagined it would be just the same for the pilot. Seat belts tight, we sat back and waited.

Bump! Bump! We were down, but the Hercules didn't settle like a normal airliner on a tarmac runway. Instead, the aeroplane shook and shuddered for the full length of the landing roll. There was also an upsurge in engine noise as the pilot applied reverse thrust. It was all over in a matter of seconds and the pilot shut down the engines and lowered the ramp at the back. Everyone was talking at once as we unstrapped our seat belts. Then came the moment I'd been waiting for.

Crampons fixed to my boots, I stepped on to the ice cap of Antarctica. The arrival was stunning. In front of me were the sheet of rippling blue ice of the runway; hundreds of square miles of white ice in every direction, broken only by the black and white of Patriot Hills rising 1,200 feet out of the ice surface; and a huge blue sky that stretched to every horizon. For a while I stopped breathing. I came back to the reality of people, luggage, and skidoos – the latter are like motorbikes on skis – and started to walk across the ice to the coloured tents of the camp, a mile distant. The crampons gave me a grip on the ice and, 25 minutes later, I took them off before I entered the blue and white mess tent, which was half hidden in a trench. Inside, 40 people milled about collecting their large plates of hot stew from the counter at the kitchen end of the long tent. I found a place at one of the wooden tables that ran alongside the central aisle of the tent and as I ate I watched the noisy, milling people – some miserable because they were leaving, others cheerful and excited because their adventure was beginning. Then I heard a strong, female voice call out, "We're going on to Vinson!" and the noise level went up.

The Branscomb Glacier

Kris, the young Canadian woman who had spoken, advanced down the mess tent advising the passengers for Mount Vinson that, as soon as we finished eating, we should sort our luggage for the onward flight. Soon she was helping me drag my rucksack and kit bag from one of the skidoo-drawn sledges across the ice to a parked Twin Otter aeroplane. High-winged and with twin jet-prop engines, it was the workhorse of Antarctica. It carried 11 passengers or a sizeable cargo. It had the same reverse thrust facility as the Hercules, with the added advantage of being fitted with skis rather than wheels. A small, orange-coloured aeroplane next to it grabbed my attention, mainly because it looked like G-AJIT. It was single-engined, a taildragger, and equipped with skis. Kris told me it was called the Polar Pumpkin and I decided there and then that I wanted to fly in it. However, that would have to wait. Two hours after we landed in Patriot Hills from Punta Arenas, we took off again for Mount Vinson Base Camp on the Branscomb Glacier.

Two Twin Otters made the journey. The one I flew in carried six passengers and most of the luggage. I had a window seat and watched as the Sentinel Range slipped past below us. 50 miles beyond it I saw the horizon where the white ice met the blue sky. I felt no fear flying over the ice – as long as the surface was suitable, the Twin Otter could land anywhere. I glanced through the windscreen, visible through the cockpit because there was no door on it. Ahead I could see a great, bare mountain wall, outlined clearly against the blue sky. "That's Mount Tyree," a voice said. At 15,918 feet, it is the second highest mountain on Antarctica; five miles to the south, on the other side of the Branscomb Glacier, is Mount Vinson. Moments before we saw it, another mountain appeared – a lovely, isolated pyramid shape, like the Matterhorn in Switzerland. Then Vinson was in view, with the Branscomb Glacier sweeping down from the top of Vinson Massif towards the Nimitz Glacier below. Too soon, we had to land on the ice, the power of the engines blowing up the spindrift when the pilot applied the reverse thrust. For several minutes I watched the tiny snowflakes turn to diamonds in the sky as they reflected the dazzling sunlight on their way groundwards. Then I turned towards the Weatherhaven tent that served as base camp for ANI.

A tall figure was standing close to the entrance and warily watching our arrival. He walked forward and extended his hand to me, "Hi! You must be Sheila Dyson. I'm Dave Hahn." I grasped his huge hand and looked into his face. He was dark haired with a luxuriant dark brown beard covering the lower half of his face. Thick dark eyebrows overshadowed his brown eyes and his physique overshadowed the people around. He was 6 feet 5 inches tall. Dressed in a navy blue thermal polar suit, he had large snow boots on his feet. He looked the part of the Antarctic mountaineer and I remembered Anne's comments from the night before.

Dave welcomed me to Vinson Base Camp but he seemed distant as he made me a coffee in the Weatherhaven tent. I felt disappointed. Afterwards we pitched a small tent for me and even though I chatted away, Dave remained quiet. I was telling him about my previous mountain experience and, in the end, said, "I'm in no rush – I've come to Antarctica to enjoy being here. I don't want to rush up the mountain and dash off. I'm here to enjoy it." Whatever was in Dave's mind, he cheered up at my words and started to open up. We were now talking each other's language and agreed on an old-fashioned approach to the mountain where I would have time to acclimatise and we would climb the mountain at a steady pace. So we decided on a rest day for the remainder of the day and to use the following day for training. It didn't matter to me that the climbers and guides who had arrived with us were already on the move. I spent the evening chatting to the crew of one of the Twin Otters which would be staying at the camp for the duration of all our expeditions. Steve King was the pilot and his engineer was called Dave. They were both Canadian, friendly and big smokers. Before I drifted off to sleep, I mused on the reason for Dave's initial distance. He'd told me he had been at the camp for a week by himself prior to our arrival. Maybe we were a massive intrusion into the peace and solitude to which he must have become accustomed. I would have felt the same in his place.

Next day, Dave and I did three things during our training session. The first was to make an agreement whereby I could fall into a crevasse because Dave could rescue me, but he couldn't fall into a crevasse because I couldn't rescue him. Essentially, I was a walker and didn't have the climbing experience to deal with that situation. The second thing we did was to rope up on the glacier for ice axe arrest practice. If either of us lost our footing, digging the ice axe into the surface was our way of stopping. So I practised falling over on the ground and forcing the long end of the axe into the surface without me falling on its sharp back end. The final thing we did was to go for a short training walk on the glacier where Dave coached me in what I called the "Step, rest, breathe!" technique. I would take a step, pause briefly at the same time as I whooshed all the air out of my lungs, and then suck in as much as I could get. The idea was to take in the maximum oxygen possible. As long as I stuck to this pattern I could keep going, but if I started to speed up, I was soon gasping for air and forced to stop. By the time we returned to camp, Dave seemed satisfied with my performance.

That evening after dinner in the Weatherhaven I produced, for Dave's inspection, the climbing gear that I'd brought from home. He watched in silence as I showed him an old Don Wilhan's seat harness and karabiner that had belonged to Cyril. I was proud of these items as, to me, they were evidence of serious climbing, even if it wasn't mine. The atmosphere became pregnant as I waited for Dave's response. He said, in gentle tones, "I think we'll leave those behind." I couldn't hide my disappointment. "Aren't they good enough?" I asked sadly. It felt like leaving Cyril behind. Dave explained, in the same gentle tones, "They're very old and the strength of the nylon in the harness will have deteriorated. And we don't know the strain the karabiner has been under. I think we'd better take some modern ones." Deflated, I looked at Cyril's equipment and then at Dave. "Would I be better to throw them away?" I asked in a sad voice. Dave answered with exquisite tact, "Save them! They have antique and historical value!" I started to laugh and the tension was broken. There was a lot of kindness in Dave Hahn.

Next day, Sunday 5 January, was the real start of our expedition. Dave showed me our proposed route on the map. From the Base Camp

G-AJIT and me, Netherthorpe Airfield, summer 1996   *Photo: S. Cullen*

Ian Drake, Netherthorpe Airfield

Photo: S. Dyson

Martyn Webster in Galway, Ireland, July 1997

Photo: S. Dyson

Branscomb Glacier, the ice fall and Mount Vinson on the right, Mount Tyree on left,
taken from the Twin Otter   *Photo: S. Dyson*

Camp 1 1/2, Branscomb Glacier, January 1997   *Photo: D. Hahn*

On the summit of Mount Vinson, 16,067 feet   *Photo: D. Hahn*

Dave Hahn, Patriot Hills   *Photo: S. Dyson*

The Polar Pumpkin, Patriot Hills   *Photo: M. Wendon*

Loading the Hercules, Patriot Hills   *Photo: S. Dyson*

we would follow the curve of the Branscomb Glacier to the top of the ice fall and, from there, follow a long steady incline to the summit ridge. Summit day would involve an ascent of 4,000 feet. We agreed to walk rather than ski, as my skiing experience was limited. My strength on the mountain lay in the fact that I was a strong, fit and experienced hill walker. I had also done a lot of backpacking. We would make three camps on the journey – Camps One and Two on the glacier, and Camp Three on the top of the ice fall, at 12,000 feet, from where we would make our attempt on the summit.

It took two hours to pack our gear. I discarded all unnecessary items, apart from Elmer the bear and my journal. Dave showed me how to stuff my down sleeping bag and clothing into my rucksack by giving them a good 'fisting'. He then offered to take any items I couldn't fit in on a sledge that he was going to pull behind him. It was starting to feel like a team effort. Late morning we set off. I shouldered my rucksack, which weighed about 25 pounds. A pound of it was a large bar of Chilean chocolate which Dave gave me and which I placed against the back of the rucksack. It was an excellent source of energy but the sight of such a large bar killed my appetite, already depressed by altitude.

We roped up and followed the tracks we had made the previous day. As we plodded on in an even rhythm, I could hear Cyril's voice, "There's only one way to 3,000 feet – slowly!" and that was how Dave and I spent the next six hours. His sledge was attached to his harness by a separate rope but it was connected to our rope by a karabiner which stopped it swinging about. The surface was solid ice and made the walking easy. Dave's main concern was crevasses, for which he kept a good lookout and which he marked with a bamboo cane every time he found one. We stopped every hour for a brief rest and gradually worked our way round the base of the ridge coming off the Vinson Massif. The slope had a gentle incline. Dave guided me away from the area where Camp One was normally sited to another site a quarter of a mile away. He said, "There seems to be new crevasses developing over there – we'll call the new site Camp One and a Half!" When we got there, he already had a food cache hidden under the ice. He said: "I've cheated a bit – I brought this up on my last trip!" I didn't mind – it was less for both of us to carry.

Dave pitched the tent, a three-man Kelty tent with two large bell ends. I watched him working in between long, greedy looks at my new environment. I couldn't see Mount Vinson's summit, but I could see the huge rock walls of Mount Tyree and the broad expanse of the Branscomb Glacier, surrounded on three sides by mountain ridges, with an open end where it fell away to meet the Nimitz Glacier 2,000 feet below. I looked at the neat yellow Kelty and thought about the slide show where I had acquired my Antarctic dream – it was a picture of a small, orange tent on the ice that had inspired me. Now I had my own. As he put in the last pegs, Dave told me to relax, muttering something about having to earn his guide money while he cooked my supper. He put a bin liner on the ice seat next to the stove and I sat on it and ate my supper with profound contentment. I thought again what a simpleton I must be, just like the time I ate the Magnum with Martyn on the roadside in Killarney. Simple things made me happy.

I slept until Dave nudged me awake at 10 am when the sun had warmed the tent. After a porridge breakfast, I repacked the bar of Chilean chocolate without opening it. Dave again pointed out its benefits, but my stomach revolted at the sight of it and I shoved it down the back of my rucksack. It was a short walk that day – only one and a half hours to Camp Two. I was surprised to find it located in a small ice gulley off the side of the glacier. I was even more surprised to find two Kelty tents already pitched there. Dave mentioned they belonged to Skip Horner's group. He pitched our tent a little way from theirs and then cooked our supper. Afterwards, we spent a long, lazy evening planning our ascent of the ice fall the following day. I also learned about Antarctic toilets at altitude. It was less sophisticated here than at Patriot Hills where a commode in a toilet tent was provided for women and a fuel barrel with a funnel for men. At Camp Two there were no concessions for women, who had to share the common pee hole in the ice marked by the inevitable bamboo cane. Dave said to me: "Everyone has to use the same spot – we don't want our ice for cooking and drinking coming from this end of the campsite!" About the ice fall, he said, "It's a dangerous place to be. There are lots of ice blocks waiting to tumble and, in between them, there's lots of crevasses. It's not a place to hang about." Relaxing in the cooling sun, it didn't look too bad to me.

We had a final cup of tea before we turned in. We were beginning to get used to each other and whenever I said "a cup o'tea" Dave would mimic my Irish Sheffield accent. I took to calling him "Big Damn Mountain Man" in an American accent. The words were written on the side of a large thermal mug that he had and everyone at ANI knew who owned it. As we sipped our tea we talked about our lives at home. I told him about Cyril and his climbing and he was a good listener. He told me of his experiences on Mount Everest, whose summit he had reached two years before. I recognised in him a profound love and respect for mountains, with an attitude to mountaineering that bordered on the puritan. He was steeped in mountaineering history, just like Cyril had been. I could imagine Cyril nodding in approval as Dave talked.

The next day was my forty-eighth birthday, and I spent it climbing the ice fall on the Vinson Massif. As I opened my eyes that morning, Dave thrust a mini Mars bar and two packets of raisins at me. He said: "Happy Birthday! Now eat!" I felt pleased that he had remembered it and I hid the Mars bar in the pocket of my rucksack. Then I gobbled the two packets of raisins before consuming a large bowl of porridge for breakfast. After that, it was all systems go and we left Camp Two at 11 am.

The wind blew thick cloud over the ice fall as we moved up the first 800 feet on the lower, gradual slope. Dave had left the sledge behind and we kept the rope well stretched out between us, but not too taut. If one of us slipped there wouldn't be much rope to run out as we dug our ice axes in. We stopped after an hour on a small ledge for a rest. I drank a pint of water and ate the nuts and raisins that Dave passed to me. Then, onwards and upwards. The angle of the ice fall increased over the next 700 feet as we moved up between lumps of fallen ice and entered an area of crevasses. After another rest, we tackled the most hazardous part of the ice fall, some hundreds of feet below the lip at the top. The broken lumps of ice were much larger and balanced at precarious angles. In between, there were numerous crevasses of unknown depth and shapes, tortured by the breaking, moving ice. Dave moved ahead with caution, constantly testing the ground ahead of him with his ice axe. I concentrated on following in his footsteps and tried to ignore the inherent threat in the shifting ice blocks. During a short pause, I looked down the ice fall and could see Skip Horner's group moving slowly up behind us.

The higher we climbed, the bigger the ice blocks became, but at last I could see the angle of steepness easing and I sensed the top was near. Dave, probably to keep me focused, said: "We're not there yet. There's still some distance to Camp Three." Minutes later we arrived. The campsite sat neatly on top of the ice fall, fixed into the side of the slope rising towards Mount Vinson which afforded a measure of protection from any winds or spindrift coming off the Massif. The campsite also gave us front line views of the biggest mountains in Antarctica. Although on one side Mount Vinson was hidden behind the long ridge that led to the summit ridge, on the other was Mount Shin, at 15,751 feet the third highest mountain on the continent. I realised it was the beautiful, solitary pyramid of a mountain that I'd seen from the Twin Otter when we arrived at Base Camp. Beyond it was Mount Epperly and beyond that was Mount Tyree, separated from Mount Vinson by a long, high level ridge. I loved what I saw but it didn't stop me feeling cold and exhausted.

As Dave pitched our tent, which he had stored in a cache on a previous trip, I walked round the new site trying to keep warm. My hands were getting colder and the feeling of exhaustion did not go away. If anything, it got worse. I felt breathless as I moved around and I had aching muscles all over my arms, legs and body. I told Dave how I was feeling but he said I was doing great and I had good reserves. That didn't make me feel any better. As soon as the tent was up, I lay down on my sleeping bag while Dave prepared the evening meal. He gave me his usual instruction: "Relax!" A few minutes later, in a private moment, I discovered that my period had started. This was the reason for my utter exhaustion as I completed the ice fall. That natural feeling compounded the other exhaustion-causing factors – altitude, cold and dehydration. The air in Antarctica is so dry that the act of breathing causes dehydration – the air I breathed out contained more moisture than the air I breathed in.

During the evening another group of climbers passed through Camp Three on their way down from the summit of Mount Vinson. They described their 13-hour long summit day. As I listened, I became increasingly depressed. I knew the exhausting effects of my period would last for a day or so and the thought of 13 hours of severe physical stress on our summit attempt the following day defeated me completely. An hour later, I fell into an uneasy sleep, anxious about how I would cope with summit day.

Summit Day

"How are you feeling?" Dave asked when I poked my head over the top of my sleeping bag next morning. His cheerful face made me miserable. I felt only marginally better for my night's sleep and, as I pulled myself out of the bag, a wave of nausea swept through me. I sat up and felt exhausted again. I hated the idea of summit day but hadn't yet worked out a way to tell Dave, so I growled at him, "All right, I suppose." He carried on with his preparations for summit day and, in the end, I decided I had to tell him. I spoke clearly, "I'd really rather have a rest day today." He turned from his rucksack and looked at me, disappointed. He said carefully: "Wait until you've had something to eat and started moving." I grunted.

A large porridge breakfast produced no change in my sick, tired, miserable feeling. Dave asked me again how I felt and I growled back: "Nauseous and tired." We grumbled on at each other and I resisted all Dave's efforts to drag me out of my low feeling. In the end, he realised I was in no mood to do the mountain and made a disappointed declaration that we would have a rest day. Even as he spoke, I felt a pang of regret and I said to him, miserably: "Am I letting you down?" He answered me directly: "No, if you'd decided to go down, I would have been, but you clearly need a rest day. Remember, whatever the weather is like tomorrow, this is a decision that we had to make. You need a rest and should have no regrets in the years to come if the weather is bad tomorrow. We're doing what is right for us now." He was right.

As soon as the decision was made, my tension started to ebb away and, as the hours passed, so did Dave's disappointment. I hated the feeling that he was disappointed, but I hated even more the prospect of a tortured and, probably, failed summit attempt. Perhaps I should have told him the full reason for my exhaustion, but I didn't because of an embarrassing experience three years before. I was the only woman on a Scottish winter mountaineering course and one of the men was a doctor who was training for a Himalayan expedition on which he would be the medical officer. At dinner one night he made public and scathing comments about women's periods being a major problem on the mountain and the disruption they caused. I wanted to take a swipe at him but didn't as I had no wish to destroy the otherwise pleasant atmosphere on the course. However, I resolved then that I would never use a period as the excuse for a poor performance. Looking back, this was foolish on Mount Vinson where it was a major factor in how I was feeling and Dave would have understood. By early afternoon we had both recovered our spirits and I was regaining my energy. We companionably made our preparations for summit day the following day. I told Dave that I felt much better for the rest and he replied, laughing: "You gave me such an accusing look over the top of your sleeping bag – a look of horror that I might actually want to go climbing!"

I was mightily relieved the next day when the good weather held for our summit attempt. A light wind would soon blow off the low cloud that hung over the top of the ice fall. We set out at 11 am and took the innocuous trail of footsteps up the steep slope behind our tent. As Dave and I fell into the "Step, rest, breathe" rhythm, I noticed Skip Horner's group getting ready to leave camp. I turned my attention back to Dave's footprints, which I was following so I didn't have to break trail for myself. He coached me to stay in rhythm because it was the most effective way of keeping going within a tolerable level of physical discomfort. On the few occasions where I tried to go faster, I would grind to a halt within seconds, gasping for breath.

After two hours we reached the top of the slope above the campsite and found ourselves on a flat area of glacier from where the body of the Vinson Massif, including Mount Vinson, rose up. The steep slope in front of us would take us directly to the summit ridge but Dave decided that, for my sake, we would walk further around the base of the mountain to a slope of easier angle. It would make our day longer, but the ascent would be less strenuous. The length of time on the ascent didn't matter as in the Antarctic summer there is daylight for the full 24 hours.

I followed Dave around the corner to the point where he had decided to start our main ascent. Just then, we converged with Skip Horner's group. I felt strangely disturbed by their presence – I'd become accustomed to the isolation of the mountain and the excellent company of my guide. I was further disturbed when I overheard a conversation between Dave and Skip. One of Skip's clients had, literally, got cold feet and had to return to Camp Three. Skip's two remaining clients were struggling and it was suggested that one of them might join our rope. I didn't want that. I didn't want our hard-won rhythm and team work disturbed by the presence of an unknown person on our rope. I said nothing and gave them no encouragement. Dave seemed to think likewise and, a few minutes later, we set off again, just the two of us. It was a good decision because, shortly afterwards, Skip's two remaining clients had to turn back.

The 3,000 feet of the long slope above were a challenge to my endurance as the increasing altitude, cold and dehydration took their toll. The few upward glances that I made to the top of the slope depressed me – for the next few hours there was nothing ahead of me except hard, physical slog. Dave pestered me to eat whenever we stopped for a rest, but my digestive system had shut down and the only thing that I could force down my dry throat was squash; but no matter how much I drank, it was never enough.

At 14,000 feet I had my crisis. During a brief rest I looked up at the endless slope and I could feel my motivation draining away. I thought of my warm bed at home and asked myself just what was I doing on this mountain. Dave knew exactly what was going on in my head and he said sternly: "It's your decision, Sheila. You can make it but you've got to work. It's up to you." In a part of myself I thought how good it would be to quit, but another part made its voice heard: "You'll only come this way once, you'll regret it for ever if you don't try." I said to Dave, "It's now or never – let's give it a go." We moved off, every part of my body yelling for mercy. For the next three hours I struggled and struggled but never again thought of quitting. Dave's words had forced me to face my own possible failure and I didn't want to fail.

Contrary to his advice, I started to find encouragement by looking to the top of the slope. Every time I glanced upwards it was a little closer and at last, after four hours of the hardest physical stress I'd ever endured, we reached the summit ridge. I went through a range of emotions as I steadied myself for the last stage of the climb – relief at being there, an awareness of how exhausted I was and a fear of the precipitous ridge with a long way to fall if I slipped off it.

Weariness made me clumsy as we proceeded along the ridge towards the summit and I caught one of my crampons on my other leg. Over I went, yelping in fear as I did so. Dave looked annoyed – false alarms caused needless stress. He growled at me and sent me on ahead so he could see exactly what I was doing.

And then we were there. The summit was on a narrow part of the ridge, a small pointed area of snow. It was not much bigger than the size of my dining room table and sloped away steeply in all directions. Dave called to me to take care. I edged my way along to the summit point and leaned one knee against it. Warily, I reached for a ski stick that had been stuck into the ice. A piece of blue nylon thread blew in the light breeze. Dave said: "That was left behind by a Chinese expedition. You always know you're on the summit of Mount Vinson when you see it. Now sit and have a rest!" I didn't need telling a second time.

I perched myself against the side of the small summit, aware that the only feelings I had were of exhaustion and relief that we had made it. I took several photographs of the world around me. Broken cloud came and went over the nearby ridges and the view down the slopes kept disappearing and reappearing. I tried to drink from my flask but the fluid was hard to swallow. Dave had moved a little way along the ridge from me and I wondered what he was doing. I found out when he returned and put something into my hand. It was a small, flat piece of brown rock and the sort of souvenir I'd have collected myself if I'd had the strength – a kind gesture by the Big Damn Mountain Man. He made another one when he took photographs of me with my camera. Then I asked him: "Which way is the South Pole?" He pointed and I pulled myself to my feet. I turned to face it and, as on Mera Peak, I raised my arms and yelled at the top of my voice, "CYRIL!" I did it a second time just to be sure. Dave gave me a thumbs up. I took a photograph of him squatting on one knee on the summit, his large physical presence filling it. He looked as though he naturally belonged there.

We both sat for a while and tried to eat. He passed me some biscuits which I forced down my throat with difficulty. The large bar of Chilean chocolate stayed in my rucksack as did the cheese and jam sandwiches that I'd made that morning. I managed to drink some orange juice as Dave moved away again. I wondered what he was up to this time. A minute later, he returned carrying a steel cylinder in his gloved hand. He squatted down next to me, unscrewed the lid and turned the cylinder upside down. Out fell a notebook and pencil. Dave passed me the notebook and said: "Open it!" Inside was a record of everyone who had reached the summit. He pointed to the place where I should sign my name and passed me the pencil. I looked at the names already recorded and Dave turned to a previous page where Chris Bonnington's name was. For about five seconds my exhaustion fell away as I added my name to the illustrious list – "Sheila Dyson, Sheffield, 9 January 1997." I could feel Cyril smiling.

We spent half an hour on the summit before starting our descent. My feet were clumsy with weariness and several times I tripped over my crampons. Dave was very patient. On one occasion I fell over and, when I tried to get up, the weight of my rucksack held me back and Dave had to haul me to my feet. On down the great slope we went, along to the more level glacier, on and on. We stopped twice for water and biscuits which I only ate because Dave placed them in my hand. What kept me going was the knowledge that if I sat down for a long rest, I would only get cold and the mountain would still be waiting for me to descend.

After three and a half hours we reached the top of the slope down to Camp Three. Dave said: "Only another half hour!" The slope seemed to stretch a long way down but soon the yellow tents appeared. My exhaustion faded enough for me to have a sense of triumph now that the journey was almost done, but it was the prospect of sitting down and not getting up again that was the best feeling of all. When we finally reached the tent at 10 pm, Dave insisted I had dinner before going to sleep. It consisted of soup, pasta and a gallon of tea. While the two of us ate, chortling to ourselves, Skip Horner appeared at the door of the tent. "Did you make it?" he asked. "Yes!" Dave answered and he and I grinned at each other. He described the cloud and temperature on the summit – –20 degrees Celsius – and Skip withdrew. I eased myself stiffly into my sleeping bag, laid my head down and remembered nothing else.

Return Journeys

Waking up was luxurious – I was cocooned in the comfort of my sleeping bag and lay there revelling in the knowledge that I had made it to the summit of Mount Vinson. I felt a huge elation. Dave was fiddling with the stove in readiness for making breakfast when the zip on the fly sheet was pulled up and Skip Horner stuck his head in the opening. He looked at me and growled, "Sheila Dyson, the guys want to know who the hell are you that you can just walk up Mount Vinson!" I said nothing, and tried to hide the large smirk on my face under the rim of my sleeping bag.

Skip was in a predicament. Two of his clients, Dean and Tom, had decided not to try again for the summit that day, but Richard, the man with the cold feet of the previous day, was keen. Skip didn't want to desert his other two clients. Dave turned to me directly and asked whether I would mind having a rest day if he took Richard up the mountain. Of course, I wouldn't – if I was in Richard's place, I would jump at a second chance. Anyway, I could sleep all day and that was just what I did. I dined out that evening for the first time in Antarctica. I combed my hair and went across to Skip's tent where I ate a large dinner while squashed up against Dean and Tom. Tom had white hair and beard and a friendly smile. Dean was a Very Important Person from a big corporation in America and his main feature was his cold, green eyes. Skip didn't say much. Two hours later Dave and Richard returned, having made the summit of Mount Vinson, and Richard had the glint of triumph in his eyes.

Next morning Dave wanted to get back to Base Camp now that we were all finished on the mountain. I was impressed by his drive and energy but was content to settle back in my sleeping bag when he declared another rest day. Outside, the weather had deteriorated into an Antarctic storm. There was a whiteout over the camp, with driving wind that blew streams of low cloud and spindrift past the tents, and freezing temperatures. As Dave melted ice for our breakfast drinks I asked him what the temperature was – –30 degrees Celsius. He went on to tell me the best way to deal with the storm. "Basically, you sit it out. You stay in your tent, sleeping, reading, chatting, writing your journal. You eat and drink, but not too much. Do your best to avoid going to the toilet. It's nasty out there!" So we passed a lazy day and spent much of it talking. I told him about Sheffield being the climbing capital of England and my life there with Cyril. He told me about his mountain guiding on Mount Ranier and Mount McKinley in Alaska and his work as a ski rescue officer at Taos in New Mexico. Then, after our evening meal, the thing I'd been dreading happened. I needed the toilet and my pee bottle was full.

With great reluctance, I eased myself out of my sleeping bag and spent 20 minutes putting on my down suit, numerous layers of socks, and my big plastic snow boots. With a wry look at Dave, I opened the fly sheet and crawled out. For his sake, I zipped it up again as fast as I could. I stood up and immediately felt danger. I could hardly see beyond the end of my arm. The low cloud, driving wind and spindrift made it almost impossible to see the footprints to the bamboo-marked pee hole. Fortunately, the gusting wind blew small gaps in the cloud and I had glimpses of the bamboo cane. I staggered the short distance and with a feeling of disgust dropped my salopettes. I had a personal speed record for emptying my bladder and pulling my clothes back up. The tents had disappeared from sight but a gust of wind made them visible again. I set off back and paused at the snow throne, the toilet on which one dealt with solid matters. It was easy at −30 degrees to persuade myself that I didn't need to use it and I hurried back to the tent. As I unzipped the fly sheet, I said to Dave, "Thank goodness I didn't have to use the snow throne!" His response was unexpected. "You fool!" he said, "You've got yourself all the way out there. Go back and do it!" I felt like a child being sent to sit on the toilet and wait for a bowel movement, but I obeyed.

Dave's words were indicative of the client/guide relationship which had developed between us. He was my guide on the mountain and my safety and well being were his responsibility. As well as actually guiding me, he needed to know that I was physically fit and well so I could perform. As a result, he constantly urged me to eat and drink more to keep up my energy and fluid levels and, it seemed, he also kept a discreet eye on my toilet performance. So back out into the storm I went and followed my footprints to the snow throne. It was cold on the throne and it felt even colder when I took my gloves off to work the toilet roll. Within five seconds, I knew the real meaning of −30 degrees as I could feel the frostbite starting. Cursing, I abandoned the toilet roll and made another record for pulling my clothes together. I scuttled back to the tent as fast as my snow boots would let me and shot in the door. I was working on the theory that it was better to be warm, dirty and alive than cold, clean and dead. I never did tell Dave about the toilet roll.

The storm had petered out by the time I woke next morning and Dave announced our early departure for Base Camp. We both packed our rucksacks and Dave returned everything to his cache of supplies buried in the ice. I felt a wave of sympathy for him as he arranged the thick black bin liner from the snow throne on the top of his sack. It was his unpleasant task to ensure it was removed from the camp and eventually transferred back to Patriot Hills for onward transport to Punta Arenas. It was one of the rules of the Antarctic Treaty that people operating on the ice should take out with them all human waste and it fell to Dave to carry out ours. Without complaint, he did his job.

I had troubles of my own on the ice fall. As soon as we came over the lip at the top, I looked down. The deep crevasses and precarious ice blocks sent a shiver of fear through me and I did what I always do when I'm worried on a mountain, I proceeded slowly, holding on tight to my trusty ice axe. As usual, I followed in Dave's footsteps while he checked the ice ahead of him with his ski stick. He sensed my fear and kept me on a short rope. Suddenly I tripped over my crampons and staggered sideways, but Dave kept the rope tight as I scrambled to my feet. The incident happened so fast that I didn't have time to dwell on it and afterwards could only concentrate on trying to avoid it happening again. During the descent through the biggest ice blocks, Dave stayed close and I found his guiding presence reassuring. At last we were through it and came to a solitary promontory of ice where he stuck his axe in and belayed me on to it. I felt secure as I ate chocolate and raisins and looked down the next stage of the ice fall which fell away at a gentler angle. Then Dave said: "Are you OK to wait here? I want to take our sacks over the next bit of steep ground – it will make it easier for both of us." I agreed.

I watched him as he fought his heavily laden way across the snow slope to my left. He returned after about 20 minutes, stepping smartly up the hill. I was feeling chilly and was glad when the sun came clear of the clouds as we set off, tight-roped, down the slope. My fear returned when, foolishly, I looked down the fall. Dave did everything he could to reassure me and I felt ashamed of my fear. He remained patient throughout and, after we had passed the last crevasse, insisted that we carry on down the slope until well clear of the last of the rock rubble. After a short rest, we carried on to Camp Two and the walking was easier on good ground. Even then, Dave's professionalism and care were evident. At Camp Two he collected his sledge on which he placed the dreaded bin liner and added to it the one from that site as well. He collected another at Camp One and a Half. As we progressed down the Branscomb Glacier to Base Camp, he kept me at the limit of my pace as well as pulling the sledge which kept swinging out of control. He'd kept it off the main rope so as not to pull me off my feet but he re-attached it when we reached the lower, gentle slope. At last the Weatherhaven tent of Base Camp came into view and automatically I straightened up and marched towards it. It was our homecoming and I was proud of what we'd done.

Steve and Dave, the aircrew of the Twin Otter, welcomed us as we walked into Base Camp. They presented each of us with a can of beer and Dave and I sat on chairs for the first time in a week. I caught sight of myself in a small mirror hanging on a nail in the tent – greasy, dishevelled hair, skin dark brown where the sun and the reflected glare from the ice had got to it, and dark circles under my eyes. Well, at least I had done something to look like this.

Life in Base Camp was a gentle anti-climax after our expedition. Dave slipped back into his role as manager and I slipped into recovery mode. While we waited for good weather for the return flight to Patriot Hills, I took my ease with long sleeps and lounging about the camp. I started making contact with the other group still in camp – the Croatians and Slovenians who had completed their Seven Summits challenge. I was drawn to two of them in particular: Victor was a bearded primary school teacher, while Stanislaus, a printer, was older with white hair. They were modest and understated about their achievements, not least of which was their ascent of Mount Everest. And on Mount Vinson they had put up a hard new route and returned to Base Camp within 27 hours. They'd spent the rest of their time extreme skiing on the Branscomb. Yet they had time for me and my achievement of walking up the mountain.

The call to fly came at 6.30 am two days later. I had been at Vinson for nearly 11 days and now I had an hour to complete my packing. The camp was alive with movement and people calling to each other as tents were dismantled. I hung round the Weatherhaven and overheard Dave talking on the radio to Patriot Hills. The Polar Pumpkin was coming with one Twin Otter to collect us. As soon as I heard that, I was in the door of the tent. "Dave, I'd like a ride in the Polar Pumpkin!"

It was the small orange-coloured taildragger aircraft I'd seen at Patriot Hills and had instantly wanted to fly in it. Dave's reply wasn't encouraging. He said: "Well, whoever rides in the Cessna is up to the pilot. Someone will have to be very assertive!" I remembered his words.

It was a beautiful morning, the sky becoming bluer and clearer as the minutes passed. Someone called out, "There it is!" as a dark, moving speck appeared in the vast expanse of the Nimitz Glacier. Gradually I recognised the shape of a Twin Otter, but its red and white colours only became visible as it turned towards us on the Branscomb. The atmosphere in camp was crisp with tension as the Twin Otter landed uphill on the glacier and the thrust from its engines blew spindrift into the air for more diamonds in the sky. Lovely as that was, I scanned the Nimitz for the Polar Pumpkin which was much harder to spot because of its smaller size. At last I saw it, and once my eyes had locked on to it, I didn't let go.

It came in lower than the Twin Otter and touched down yards away from where I stood with Dave, its tail ski remaining high until it had lost all its flying speed and then sinking gracefully on to the ice. The Pumpkin soon slowed on the uphill slope and the pilot taxied it in close to camp. I followed Dave as he strode across the ice to greet the pilot. His words took me by surprise, when I heard him say loudly, "Max, Sheila Dyson's hot to fly with you!" Max Wenden, the bearded New Zealand pilot, had barely swung himself out of the door when Dave said again, "Max, Sheila Dyson's hot to fly with you!" I could have kissed him.

I watched while the outgoing Otter was loaded with piles of luggage, but I kept an even closer eye on Max as he drank tea with Dave. The turn-around was swift. Even as Max drained his mug, I had to say a sad farewell to the Big Damn Mountain Man. Dave enveloped me in a massive bear hug and I felt the wrench of leaving one of the finest mountain men I'd ever known. In other circumstances, he was someone I'd have wanted to get to know much, much better. I turned and gave him a quick wave as I followed Max across the ice to the Polar Pumpkin. I saw Skip Horner coming across to join us and, as we neared the aircraft, Max asked, "Who's going in the front seat?" "I WANT THE FRONT SEAT!" I almost yelled. Dave's words about being assertive were right at the front of my mind. Then I remembered my manners and turned to ask Skip, "Do you mind, Skip?" He said, sardonically, "Sheila, I wouldn't dream of arguing with you!" So it was accomplished.

Max handed me a headset as I climbed into the right-hand seat. A colleague of Max's, called Anne, who worked at Patriot Hills, and Skip were sitting in the back. Max checked my harness and slammed his door, then fired up the engine. I busied myself putting a new film in my camera, heart pumping madly.

Max went through his checks, including his radio check and I was sorry when I realised that I couldn't hear the external radio calls on my side and that there was only one set of controls. I watched every move Max made as he lined the Pumpkin up for a downhill take-off. We bumped along on skis as Max pushed the stick forward and brought the tail up. Then he tugged back gently on the stick and we were off.

The excitement almost overwhelmed me as we climbed out over the Branscomb Glacier and then turned back towards the camp, gaining altitude. We had to circle around for several minutes until the Twin Otter took off and caught us up, as we were going to fly in formation for part of the journey back to Patriot Hills. As we climbed higher, the mountains of the Sentinel Range moved slowly past my window. There were black, rocky summits with snow clinging to broad faces and glaciers rolling down the cols between them. I admired one pyramid shaped summit stretching skywards and then felt serene as it slipped from view and another bulkier summit took its place. But I had no urge to be back on the ice trying for another summit. A deeper serenity took hold of me as I realised that I was here among the highest mountains on the continent and I had stood on top of the highest.

Then I saw Max talking into his mouthpiece. A few seconds later the Twin Otter appeared on the end of my wingtip. The sun glinted on its red and white paint work and its three landing skis dangled under its wings and nose. Beneath its fuselage hundreds of square miles of ice stretched away. I watched the Twin Otter rise and fall slightly on its flight path. I knew it would be flying slowly in order to keep with the Polar Pumpkin, whose cruising speed was considerably less and I could feel the Pumpkin's engine working hard to keep up. We flew together for several minutes and then the Twin Otter banked away from us and we were alone. The flight in the Polar Pumpkin got better and better for me. It was as though I'd written a letter to God asking for a perfect flight in Antarctica, and he had answered.

181

It was a perfect flying day. We flew south, following the spiny ridge of the Sentinel Range. Through the windscreen I could see the Heritage Range in the distance. The mountains rose blackly out of the flat ice and to either side of them the ice cap stretched 70-100 miles to the horizon. Through my side window I saw the sharp, serrated ridge of the Sentinels sweep past. Just below the black top of the knife-edge ridge, the snow hung down the wall all the way to the Ellen Glacier below. At one point the ridge turned away sharply to the left and rose to a high, pointed summit. It felt as though we were close enough to see footprints in the snow where people had climbed to it, although I knew these were virgin mountains. The air was still and gave a silk-smooth ride, and there was nothing to blow us either into the ridge or away from it. The startling clarity made the extraordinary visibility possible, and as we flew on we could see the lower peaks of the Ellsworth Mountains and beyond them the ice that stretched all the way to the South Pole. In all my dreams of Antarctica, I never envisaged a flight like this.

I wouldn't even describe the flight as magical: it was beyond that. Perhaps it was because the flight pulled together the focus and passion of my three dreams. First, I'd gone to see Mount Everest and climbed my own mountain. Second, I'd become a pilot and found G-AJIT, and third, I'd made my journey on the ice and climbed Mount Vinson. On the flight in the Polar Pumpkin, all three dreams came together: high mountains, a small taildragger aircraft and the vastness of Antarctica.

Three-quarters of the way through the flight my film ran out, so I sat there and absorbed the last minutes of the journey. In a strange way, part of me was glad when it ended – the intense feeling was exhausting

– and I came back to the reality of landing on the taxiway at Patriot Hills. Max taxied the Pumpkin into a spot next to the Twin Otter. In silence, I climbed out to bright sunshine.

While Max tied the aircraft down, Anne, Skip and I trudged across the snow to the mess tent. My mind still in a whirl, I went down the ice steps and pushed the door open. As the three of us walked in, there was a round of applause and a cheer. The tent was filled with climbers and ANI staff and, down near the cooking area, a large blackboard had been balanced on a table. On it were words of welcome and congratulations to the Vinson adventurers and, to my pleasant surprise, the words "Happy Birthday, Sheila!" for my birthday the week before. A cake with lighted candles was produced and everyone sang "Happy Birthday!" The champagne corks popped and I sat there glowing with satisfaction. There's just something about Antarctica …

Patriot Hills

Once the effects of the champagne wore off, I had the task of settling in at Patriot Hills for the 10-day extension to my journey on the ice. Initially, I had a sense of anticlimax – I knew it would be different from being on Vinson and I'd have to adapt to a new set of people. I was helped by Kris, who found me a Kelty tent which we pitched about 50 yards from the mess tent. She disappeared into a nearby store tent and emerged dragging a thick foam mattress across the ice. I would be well insulated in my tent and, despite my temporary longing to be back in the rugged, isolated conditions on Vinson, I started to settle into the specialised community of Patriot Hills camp – with surprising results. There was so much of interest that even thoughts of Cyril faded into the background.

In the mess tent, I spoke to Steve Pinfold, the deputy camp manager who came from Cornwall, and arranged to go cross-country skiing with him the next morning. I met him at the underground hangar where the Polar Pumpkin lived during the winter. The hangar had been dug out of the ice and went far enough into it to cover the full length of the fuselage and the width of the wings at the front. In a corner of the hangar was a wood-lined workshop where Steve fitted me with cross-country skis but, despite his best efforts to instruct me and an enjoyable trip on the ice, I only went once. I prefer walking and flying.

Aviation was back on the agenda in the early afternoon when I sidled up to Steve King, the Twin Otter pilot who had done duty at Vinson Base Camp. He offered to show me the flight deck where he took me through the controls and instruments. He took slow, lazy drags on his cigarette as he talked to me, belying his reputation as a highly skilled bush pilot. Back in the mess tent, people were talking about the arrival of the Hercules when the runway had been cleared of snow by a solitary tractor working a small snow blower. We didn't know then it would take two days to do the work.

Next morning I clung to the safety bars of Kris's skidoo as we drove six miles across the ice to view the wreck of a DC-6, which had had to make a forced landing four years earlier due to bad weather at Patriot Hills. It was buried up to its windscreen under tons of spindrift and only the top of the fuselage, tail and windscreen were visible, along with the end of a bent propeller. There was something desolate about the broken aeroplane and I was glad to leave it behind in the gloom as we sped back to camp. When we got there, we found the place alive with chat and milling people – the Hercules had taken off from Punta Arenas and would reach Patriot Hills that evening.

At 8 pm I stood at the threshold of the ice runway with members of the ANI staff. Duncan, the bearded camp manager from Huddersfield, was holding up an anemometer to measure the wind speed. He passed that information to the pilot of the Hercules through his hand held radio, and that was the limit of aviation technology at Patriot Hills. Then I spotted a glint of light high in the sky. As it came nearer, I saw the dark shape of the Hercules surrounding it. It was a moment to marvel at – out of the huge Antarctic sky, over thousands of square miles of ice, the aeroplane had found its way to us and would ultimately carry us all home. I watched it as it glided past to touch down and then the engines roared with reversed energy and the Hercules slowed down. It was another successful arrival, and everyone was laughing and talking at once.

I watched as the new visitors stood bewildered on the ice. I knew how they felt. Then I heard a familiar voice with a warm Liverpool accent. It was Joan Elms, the lady from the ANI office in England. She had arrived with Faye, Anne Kershaw's assistant, and the two of them had the excitement of being on a very exotic office outing. They would return to Punta Arenas in two hours on the Hercules. As we walked to the camp, Faye said, "Everyone in the office was rooting for you. We were thrilled to hear you'd done Vinson. Well done!" Faye's words made me aware of the warm support of the women and it really pleased me. I was also surprised, although I shouldn't have been – I was the only woman on the mountain and was of no account to anyone in terms of mountaineering. Perhaps it was the British habit of supporting the underdog.

Once the Hercules had taken off on its return journey, carrying away the people who had arrived with me, I had a chance to inspect the newcomers in the mess tent. The climbers were already winging their way to Vinson, including a Canadian woman called Tobin Anderson, who was a breast cancer survivor. In the mess tent the most striking person to me was Ann White, a woman in her sixties who came from Taunton, Somerset. Small and thin, she didn't lack spirit. She had come for a flight to the South Pole.

The following day I did my first walk at Patriot Hills and found a major difference between them and Mount Vinson. In Patriot Hills, whenever we reached the ridge that joined the 1,200 feet summits together, a strong wind came howling across the glacier that separated our hills from the Independence Hills a mile away. It blew hard into our faces, throwing up endless spindrift. The hills themselves had steep sides in places with loose, broken rocks and being able to see only a few feet in front of me made me nervous. I was glad when we descended but the walk had one unexpected outcome.

As I trudged uphill, I was overtaken by a man named Lewis. About 40, he had the comfortable physique of a man who was not devoted to fitness. Curious, he asked me what it had been like on Vinson. So I told him about the Branscomb Glacier, the ice fall and summit day. He listened with interest and in turn caught mine when he said: "I shared a room in Punta Arenas with an Irish mountaineer called Patrick Falvey who was very keen to make the first Irish ascent of Mount Vinson." Inwardly, I chuckled. I'd done it the previous week.

As the days passed I started to spend more time with the ANI staff. In comparison to the newcomers I felt like an old timer on the ice and on Sunday 19 January had a chance to be really involved – it was the day for the flight to the South Pole.

Ann White appeared in the mess tent almost drowning in a down salopette and jacket. Her thin hair was covered by a brown hood lined with thick fur. She sat next to me, eyes gleaming with excitement. She told me that she had travelled extensively with her husband who had died a few years before. She had decided to keep travelling and a previous trip had taken her to the North Pole. Her words so belied her apparent fragility.

Two Twin Otters were to make the journey. The first, piloted by a Canadian called Jim, took off after lunch. His task was to collect from the South Pole the people that I called the 'polar travellers' – those who had been trying to make extended journeys on the ice. It was close to the end of the summer season and time to withdraw. The second Twin Otter, piloted by Steve King, set off an hour later carrying the ANI clients, including Ann White. I envied her, but there was no need. Fran Orio, the assistant cook, was doing radio watch for the flight and invited me to join her in the radio shack. And I went all the way to the South Pole on the radio.

Fran came from Walkley in Sheffield, just six miles from where I lived. She was in her third season at Patriot Hills and her kindly, cheerful nature ensured that she was well liked in camp. She had volunteered to radio follow the South Pole flights in the radio shack which was a red Weatherhaven tent with a white wooden door. Inside there was a porch with another door that led into the radio room itself. There was a long table, on which the radio rested, and two chairs. An oil heater, carefully placed, kept the tent warm.

Most flying in Antarctica is bush flying. There are few radio navigation beacons to help pilots on their way and they use a GPS (Global Positioning System) or, if that fails, astro navigation by the sun and stars. A backup for flights was the radio by which people on the ground could keep track of where the aeroplane was and the state of the flight. Accordingly, Jim and Steve would radio in every 30 minutes with their position and fuel endurance. In between the reports Fran told me of a previous trip where they'd landed in the Thiel mountains to refuel and had to dig the fuel drums out of the snow because they'd been buried in a storm.

After two hours, Duncan came into the radio shack as he wanted to contact the South Pole. It felt like history in the making as I listened to him speaking to Marek Kaminsky, a Polish man who had been attempting to cross Antarctica on skis, from Hercules Inlet to McMurdo Sound. I heard the pain in Marek's voice as he made the decision to end his attempt because the season was now too far advanced for the distance to be covered. If he had succeeded, his name would have been in the history books forever, but even his failed attempt would be recorded. I stayed in the radio shack until dinner and, later, trudged through the wind and spindrift back to my own tent for a restless night while we waited for the return of the Otters from the South Pole.

The first one came in at 6.30 am carrying Marek and the other polar travellers. Avid with curiosity, I found a quiet spot in the mess tent to watch their entrance. The first person through the door was a woman. Radiating strength and fitness, Laurence de la Ferriere, a French mountain guide, had become the third woman in the world to ski solo to the South Pole. Full of her adventure, her lively brown eyes conveyed her passion and satisfaction for what she had achieved. In contrast, Marek made a sad figure. He was well over six feet tall with long limbs and large hands and feet. His drooping posture and sad expression reflected his unfinished journey. After him came a team of Koreans, all dressed in orange down suits and led by Mr Ho. Like Marek, they had attempted to cross the ice cap, with a similar ending.

For two hours, the mess tent was filled with the excited voices of people who had been out on the ice doing things the rest of us could only dream about.

After dinner that night, the travellers each gave a talk about their journey. Everyone was silent while Laurence described her weeks of isolation as she hauled her sledge across the ice and approached the South Pole. She told us, "Then I came close to the base and, as I skied in, everyone came out to watch. But no one said a word. I couldn't understand it. I skied on with my sledge until I got to the geographical South Pole – there's a big flag marking it. I stood near it and took my harness off and threw it on the ground. Then the people came forward and made me very welcome. Later, I realised their silence was respect." I could feel the hairs standing up on the back of my neck. After that, the men's stories had a lesser impact and that night I dreamt of pulling my own sledge and marching triumphantly into the base at the South Pole.

So passed my days and nights at Patriot Hills. The season was close to its end and, even in my tent, I could feel the temperatures lowering each night. There were more spells of bad weather and the atmosphere in the mess tent on the evening of 23 January had an edge to it. People were sad at the thought of leaving Antarctica, but there was also an air of uncertainty about the arrival of the Hercules the next day. The man who ran the computer in the weather tent had forecast an extended spell of stormy weather within 48 hours. As for me, my thoughts were homeward bound.

I spent most of 24 January slumming in the mess tent with two emaciated Koreans, watching while they consumed multiple plates of

English fried breakfast, followed by multiple servings of tea and scones at eleven and double portions of lamb stew at lunch. They were repairing the severe weight loss of their expedition. The weather reports for the flight of the Hercules were unfavourable and I went to bed late with the exhausted feeling that comes from doing nothing all day.

At breakfast next morning, a loud cheer went up – the Hercules would arrive at 2 pm. The lively chatter quickly died away as everyone went out to finish their packing. Once I'd done mine, I set off across the snow to the underground hangar where Max Wenden was servicing the Polar Pumpkin before storing it for the winter. I wanted to spend my last hours in Antarctica close to the aeroplane that had given me one of the finest hours of my life. I loitered with intent until Max put a screwdriver in my hand and set me to unscrewing the pod underneath the Pumpkin's belly. He tolerated my unmechanical presence until we had released the pod and carried it across to the hangar where he secured it. Then he suggested tactfully that I go and make sure my bags were placed for loading on to the Hercules. Sadly, I said farewell to the Pumpkin. Its engine cowlings were off and it looked forlorn as it stood with its engine exposed. On one side of the fuselage, just behind the engine, the names of Giles Kershaw, Dan Weinstein and Max Wenden were painted – the ANI pilots who had the unique experience of flying it. I kept looking back at it as I walked away.

"It's coming!" The words signalled the start of a major exodus from the camp after lunch. I found Dave Hahn near the mess tent (he'd come into camp on the last Twin Otter from Mount Vinson two days before) and made my final farewell. He gave me one of his bear hugs – his arms seemed long enough to go round me twice. A final photograph, a lump in my throat and I took myself off. I could hear the steady hum of the Hercules engines on final for the ice runway. Despite the gathering clouds, Patriot Hills was still visible. The atmosphere was filled with heavy engine noise and spindrift as the aeroplane touched down and slowed to a halt. Everyone cheered as the pilot shut the engines down. The Hercules' arrival meant we could go home before the next batch of severe weather closed in on the camp.

Out at the Hercules, people were milling around. Steve and Jim of Twin Otter fame were helping to load the aeroplane. Dave Hahn was helping too and he called across to me to take my crampons off before I boarded the Hercules. I waved a cheery acknowledgement. Ann, the camp doctor, was there, Roz and Fran, the amazing cooks, Kris, the humorous Canadian – they were all there to wave us goodbye. Tobin Anderson was there, too. She had climbed Mount Vinson with Dave and she walked up the ramp with a tangible air of confidence. Then it was my turn. All goodbyes said, I stepped on to the ramp and off Antarctica. Now that the moment had come, I was content to be going home and that contentment stayed with me for the next six hours. I seated myself next to a man called Geoff Somers who had been supervising a young people's group who had come into camp. Moments later, the ramp was raised and I turned to watch it lock into position. Barrels, sledges, boxes and rucksacks were piled high at the back of the fuselage, secured by belts. Then number one engine started to turn and the aeroplane vibrated gently. The vibration increased as the remaining engines fired up and the aeroplane sat there like an angry beast waiting to pounce. It started to move towards the centre of the ice runway for take-off and I felt a constriction in my throat. The pilot gave full throttle and soon we were climbing out into thick cloud and Antarctica was gone.

I sank back into numb slothfulness. Once on the journey I looked around at the other passengers and a phrase 'the best in the world' kept coming into my mind. On this aeroplane were some of the best climbers and guides, the best explorers and travellers and the best support workers in the world and I was with them. For a short time, I had been part of their company and I'd come through. An aura of peace surrounded me – some deep part of me was satisfied. As much as Mera Peak and the Himalayas had been for Cyril, Antarctica was for me, my gift to myself. Suddenly, I was pulled from my thoughts by a touch on the shoulder. The flight engineer was standing in the aisle. "The Captain says, would you like to take his seat?" With thudding heart and heavy mountain boots, I climbed the spiral metal staircase to the flight deck.

Phil, the co-pilot, welcomed me and indicated the empty left hand seat. Grinning, I eased myself into the Captain's place. Phil depressed the radio-transmit button on his control column and spoke to the radio room in the ANI office in Punta Arenas, "Sheila has taken over as Captain!" It was Sue who answered and I piped up, "Sue, I've come up here to supervise!" Phil laughed in the right hand seat but, as I turned to speak to him, I knocked off the autopilot. Calmly, he put it back on and then showed me the various normal ways it could be disconnected. He also showed me the Horizontal Situation Indicator and asked me to move the direction needle a little to the right. I did so with enthusiasm and a magical thing happened – the aeroplane banked its wings and started to turn right. I was moving the Hercules! Phil said, "Be gentle!" A little later he asked me to make another adjustment and nodded in approval as the Hercules eased back on heading. Then he took me through every control on the flight deck, along with the gauges and different systems. He was supported by the engineer and technician chipping in with information. It was a feast of aviation. I treated Phil and the others to a description of G-AJIT and how he came down final at 45 knots. Phil laughed at my enthusiasm. Then the Captain returned and I had to vacate his seat. As I made for the spiral stairs, he shook my hand, "Congratulations on climbing Mount Vinson!"

The Captain gave me one final treat – I was allowed back on to the flight deck for the approach and landing into Punta Arenas. I stood behind his seat watching the coast of Chile slipping past in a darkening evening – the first shades of darkness I'd seen for three weeks, apart from the gloom of storms on the ice cap. It took 20 minutes of gradual descent before Punta Arenas airport appeared in the windscreen. I bent my knees so I could watch the approach from the eye level of the pilot – we were now on long final. Phil did the landing and I heard the familiar racket of reverse thrust as the aeroplane touched down smoothly on the concrete runway – I looked over at him and grinned: "Ten out of ten, Phil!" He looked pleased. Then it was time for me to go.

Anne Kershaw, Faye and Joan Elms gave each of us a hug of welcome as we stood on the tarmac and the Hercules was unloaded.

Ann White, wearing the same fur hood that she'd worn to the South Pole – where she had the time of her life – now appeared at my elbow and asked, "Was that you landing the Hercules?" For a second I was tempted to lie, but I was honest and said no.

Cabos des Hornos hotel was a world away from the ruggedness of Antarctica. I hadn't washed for three weeks as, once I'd discovered that you don't smell in Antarctica because it's too cold for the bacteria which cause bodily odour, I'd abandoned all thoughts of braving the freezing wash tent. But now I revelled in the thought of soaking in a hot bubble bath. Unfortunately, in my anxiety to put the plug in, I knocked the tooth glass off the side of the sink and it smashed in smithereens on the bottom of the bath. It took 15 minutes to clear it before, clutching a glass of beer from the room fridge, I could wallow in comfort. Then I slept.

On my last night in the city I met the ANI staff and the Hercules crew for dinner in a smart restaurant and had a strange feeling of disconnection from them all. It was as though the last threads binding me to them were unravelling and tomorrow I would break my own trail for the journey home. The best moment of the evening was when Phil, the co-pilot, presented me with a small gold brooch of a Hercules. It was like Dave giving me my piece of rock from Mount Vinson – an object of value and hard earned. I withdrew early from the dinner, overcome by a feeling of emotional disorientation, being neither in Antarctica nor home in Sheffield. Tomorrow couldn't come fast enough.

Epilogue

Sheffield had never seemed so welcoming as when I climbed into a black taxi at Midland railway station dragging my large rucksack and German army kit bag after me. The driver said: "Where have you been?" "Antarctica," I replied. "What were doing down there?" he persisted. So I told him about Mount Vinson. "Did you have a television crew? Will you be on the telly?" he asked. His Sheffield accent and direct interest made me feel glad to have something to talk about and equally glad to be telling it in Sheffield. That feeling stayed with me.

My mother welcomed me with open arms and told me how, at her weekly art classes in the Graves Gallery, she and her friends had followed my journey with the aid of a school atlas. I thought how blessed I was to have her. The warmth and comfort of home, especially hot baths and interior sprung mattresses, felt luxurious, as did sitting on regular chairs and at regular tables. And returning to work at the airfield was a pleasure. I received a warm welcome from my work mates, who were quick to tell me that I was much better tempered than I had been before I went. The thing they had most missed about me was my door slamming habit – every time I shut the back door of the flight centre, the wooden walls shook with the shock waves. I soon had a check ride to fly G-AJIT again and before long I was flying over the Derwent Valley, imagining I was passing over the icy landscape of the Ellsworth Mountains.

Two weeks after my return, in a bid to find out if I had made the first

Irish ascent of Mount Vinson, I contacted the Mountaineering Council of Ireland in the person of Joss Lynam, who operated from a house in Dublin. When I told him about my ascent of Mount Vinson, I heard a strangled laugh at the other end of the phone. "Is there a joke?" I asked, taken aback. In a serious tone, Joss informed me that an attempt on Mount Vinson had been funded by the Irish government, and had taken place two weeks after mine. So, I had got there first. I wrote a brief, formal report for *Mountain Log*, the publication of the Mountaineering Council of Ireland. It was published two months later and made the cover as 'Antarctica is News!' Patrick Falvey wrote a glowing account of his ascent two weeks after mine. Cyril would have been so proud. Then I had time to reflect on the events of the last four years and where they had taken me.

Two words summed up the effects on me of fulfilling the three dreams – contentment and confidence. The urgent desire to pursue a major goal was gone, mainly because I had achieved what was most dear to me. I had the same feeling in Sheffield that I had as I circled the mountains surrounding the Branscomb Glacier in the Polar Pumpkin – that I was content with what I had done and could rest easy. Beyond contentment there was confidence, the real legacy of the three dreams and, to see how that had come about, I had to examine each in turn.

The Himalayan trip seemed to allow the release of feelings. The intensity of fear that I felt in Dubai and Kathmandu had taken me by surprise, but it seemed to be a symptom of the aloneness that I felt. If trouble had come, there was no one to help me but myself. This feeling was exaggerated in the extreme loneliness at Khare and yet, in extremity, I did help myself. That knowledge gave me a hard kernel of confidence. The surge of emotion on Mera Peak, especially when I gave the mountain to Cyril, was an act of love. It was my gift to him. The heartache, the physical and mental effort, and the achievement, hadn't been for me, but for him; but I didn't know that until I stood facing Mount Everest. It was my tribute to Cyril and it touched the heart of what we were together.

Flying was the activity through which I built a new life for myself in Sheffield. Learning to fly brought me new inspiration and joy and gave me a piece of the Himalayas over Worksop on a Wednesday afternoon. A year after I started flying, the part-time job I took in the flight centre not only provided me with interesting work in a place that I had come to love but also brought me into contact with male company, something I had missed terribly. I was back in the mainstream of human life. And G-AJIT gave me pride and pleasure in flying.

Antarctica was the icing on the cake. It was while I was there that I realised I had pursued my dreams in the right order. The Himalayas gave me the experience of big mountains and G-AJIT gave me a deep appreciation of the adventure of flying. Antarctica combined both of these to give me one of the finest hours of my life when I made the flight in the Polar Pumpkin. It also confirmed and brought to the front of my mind the inner confidence that had been growing for the previous four years. Finally, it brought me a sense of wholeness that I had not before possessed.

I had gone to Antarctica to test myself, just like the other people going down there. I had climbed Mount Vinson with the help of my guide, Dave Hahn, as had the others with the help of theirs. I discovered that I was not the only private pilot there – several of the other climbers were as well. I had a successful teaching and lecturing career spanning twenty years and the others also had successful careers either in business or a profession. And all the 'others' were men. This made me think of my father. His repressive attitude, which had so marked my early life, was now irrelevant. The male world from which he had tried to exclude me, only to make me intensely curious, was now wide open to me, and I had taken my place in it. Not only that, I enjoyed it and revelled in it. Most important, I didn't have to be the best at anything: I only had to take part. I learned the value of so-called 'achievements' in such an environment. In Antarctica, climbing the mountain is not the big issue – successful living in Antarctica means adapting to the environment, dealing with what nature throws at you and enjoying the company of the people there. I think I managed most of that. Antarctica had brought me full circle, back to myself.

There is not much else to say except to offer a few thoughts on the nature of dreams. The first is that everyone should have a dream and, whatever happens, hold on to it. It does not matter how outrageous the dream seems – it belongs to us. Secondly, we should follow it up. We may, for a while, be able only to take small steps but, if we persist, one day we will be able to take all the steps necessary. Thirdly, despite the obstacles that seem to be in our way, if we work towards our dream, life itself will present us with opportunities. The only thing required is that we are ready to take them and, if we have been working towards our dream, we will be. Finally, following a dream takes courage, mainly because other people have a habit of telling us that we are not entitled or worthy or capable. We are.

If we do follow our dream, life not only presents opportunities, but actually rewards us, and we will find that the reality of the dream is greater that the dream itself. In the Himalayas, I was closer to Mount Everest than I had ever dreamt I would be, especially on the Ama Labsta where I was only seven miles away. The ascent of Mera Peak (21,247 feet) allowed me to claim my own Himalayan summit – this was not part of my dream. As a result of learning to fly, and gaining my Private Pilot's Licence, I became part owner of G-AJIT – yet aircraft ownership was not part of the flying dream. Lastly, when I dreamt of making a journey on the ice cap of Antarctica, I never thought I would climb the highest mountain on the continent, making it the first Irish ascent, nor that I would have a chance to fly in a single-engined aeroplane over the icy wilderness.

And what of Cyril? His death was the trigger for the fulfilment of the three dreams and he was with me on each journey, adventure and flight. He was with me as I struggled to rebuild my life. The four-year period of the dreams put a time and physical distance between me and the pain of losing him and, by the time they were accomplished, the emotional wounds were healing, and I had the feeling that I was back to normal, everyday life. The gaping wound of bereavement was no longer sapping my energy. Instead, my life had come to a place of contentment and confidence. I knew that Cyril would be part of my being for as long as I existed, whether in this life or the next, if there is one. That thought is the most healing of all.

And what next? With new confidence, I gradually assembled another three dreams. Three is a nice, round number and it gives me short- and long-term possibilities. And what are they? To have a book published, to travel on the Trans-Siberian Railway and to fly a light aircraft to Australia. They are just as crazy as the first three, but so what? If you are reading this, I am on my way!